"We're All Here at Cougar Camp . . . "

Without warning, the lights went out. Marybeth gasped in the sudden blackness.

"Somebody get a flashlight," a voice called.

Marybeth heard someone stumbling across the floor. Someone else giggled nervously.

Suddenly a brilliant flash of lightning illuminated the faces of the girls. They looked blue and bloodless. A whole room full of ghosts.

Thunder crashed.

Marybeth felt as if she were trapped in a nightmare. Her heart whammed against her ribs, making her paper costume whisper, "Ghost, ghost, ghost." Where was the light? She didn't want to, but she knew she was going to scream.

Twice she screamed. "Turn on a light," she shrieked. "I'm afraid of the dark."

Now everybody knew it . . .

BOOKS BY LAEL LITTKE

From Deseret Book

Bee There Series
1. *Getting Rid of Rhoda*
2. *The Mystery of Ruby's Ghost*
3. *Star of the Show*
4. *There's a Snake at Girls Camp*

Where the Creeks Meet

From Other Publishers

Tell Me Where I Can Go
Trish for President
Shanny on Her Own
Loydene in Love
Prom Dress
Blue Sky
The Watcher
The Peanut Butter Pond Series (6 books)
The Tall Tale Series (6 books)

THERE'S A SNAKE AT GIRLS CAMP

LAEL LITTKE

Published by
Deseret Book Company
Salt Lake City, Utah

With special thanks again to Elizabeth Long.

© 1994 Lael Littke

Library of Congress Cataloging-in-Publication Data

Littke, Lael.
    There's a snake at Girls Camp / Lael Littke.
        p.   cm. — (The Bee Theres : bk. 4)
    Summary: The Bee Theres try to find ways to earn money so that they can go to summer camp, while Marybeth worries that camping will expose her secret fear of the dark.
    ISBN 0-87579-845-4
    [1. Camps—Fiction. 2. Fear of the dark—Fiction. 3. Moneymaking projects—Fiction.— 4. Mormons—Fiction.] I. Title. II. Series: Littke, Lael. Bee Theres : bk. 4.
PZ7.L719Th 1994   94–751
[Fic]—dc20   CIP
                                 AC

Printed in the United States of America

10 9 8 7 6 5 4 3 2 1

For Arthella, a truly happy camper

CHAPTER
1

Marybeth's mother had a bumper sticker on her car that read "I can handle anything. I have children."

Marybeth had always totally believed this was true. If there was anybody who was unflappable in any situation, it was her mom. There were eight kids in Marybeth's family, and her mom said frequently that she specialized in emergency and disaster management.

That's why Marybeth was so startled the morning she looked out of her bedroom window and saw Mom sitting on the Limbo Limb, high in the huge, spreading oak tree in front of their house. She was dressed in her yellow jogging outfit, as if she'd gone out for a run but ended up, somehow, in the tree.

"Mom!" she yelled, although she knew her

mother couldn't hear her. "What are you doing up there?"

The Limbo Limb was a thick branch high in the big tree where Marybeth and her brothers and sisters had always gone when they needed to think through a problem, or when they were in some kind of a pickle, or when they were indulging in a little private pity party. It was hard to get up to the Limbo Limb, which Mom had always said was one of the benefits of going there. "There is no strength where there is no struggle," she'd say.

You had to struggle, all right, to get up to the Limbo Limb. You had to shinny up the tree trunk, fling a leg over the lowest branch, then hoist yourself up to where you could get some footing to climb the rest of the way.

How had Mom got up there? She was over forty years old. How could a person her age shinny, fling, and hoist her way up to the Limbo Limb? But most important, why?

Marybeth dressed quickly and was just about to run downstairs when the telephone rang. Somebody answered on one of the extensions in the big house and bayed, "Marybeth. It's for you-hoo."

That had to be Garth, one of the fourteen-year-old twins. He was the only person in the family who said things with an echo.

Marybeth ran to the hall extension and picked it up. "Hello," she said, craning her neck to look through her sister Katie's room and on out to the Limbo Limb, where her mother sat gazing off into the distance. What was she looking at?

"Hi, Marybeth." It was Carlie on the phone. She was one of the girls in Marybeth's Beehive class. "I was just wondering what I need to bring to the meeting today."

"Meeting?" Marybeth walked into Katie's room as far as the phone cord would allow her to go. Now her mother's head was bent down and she seemed to be reading something. Or writing maybe? Could she be knitting? There was a leafy branch in the way, so Marybeth couldn't see what she had on her lap.

Why would she be doing *any* of those things up in the tree?

"Yeah, meeting," Carlie said. "The Bee Theres meeting at your house. *You* know. We're going to talk about going to girls camp."

"Oh, the meeting." Marybeth remembered now that the other Bee Theres, which was a club the girls in her Beehive class had formed, were coming to her house right after lunch. She remembered too that before she got out of bed and saw her mother in the tree, she'd been trying to think up a way to tell the others she wouldn't be going to girls camp. She had been thinking they would want to know why she wasn't going. How could she explain why?

"The meeting," she repeated.

"Marybeth," Carlie said, "is something wrong?"

"No," Marybeth said quickly. "It's just, y'know, I kind of forgot." Should she tell Carlie that she couldn't have the meeting at her house? Would her mom be down out of the tree by then? What would her friends think if they came and saw her up there? Nobody else's mother sat up in trees.

"I'm excited about girls camp," Carlie went on. "Do you think it will be as much fun as it sounds?"

"Probably," Marybeth said. It didn't matter whether it was or whether it wasn't. She wasn't going.

"Do you have any ideas for earning our money for camp?" It didn't seem as if Carlie would ever stop talking. Marybeth wanted her to hang up so she could hurry outside and find out what was going on with Mom.

Outside she saw her little sister Katie come down the street with a couple of her eight-year-old friends. They all stopped underneath the big tree, and their mouths hung open as they looked up to where Mom sat gazing at something far away. "No, I don't have any ideas," Marybeth said into the phone. "We'll, y'know, talk about it later. 'Bye, Carlie."

She didn't even wait for Carlie to say goodbye.

Slamming down the phone, she ran downstairs and through the living room to the front door. She wondered if she should call Dad, who was a psychiatrist. He might know what was wrong with Mom.

Garth and Grant, the twins, were in the living room, lifting weights. They scattered their dumb equipment throughout the whole house so that a person was apt to fall over a barbell just about anywhere.

"Come outside," Marybeth said. "Mom's up on the Limbo Limb."

"So-ho?" Garth said.

Marybeth stopped. "What do you mean, *so*? She's up in the *tree*, goofy. She must be having some kind of, y'know, *crisis*."

"Yip," Grant said.

Marybeth felt a moment of fury. Grant and Garth had decided they were going to break her of the habit of saying "y'know" so much, so every time she said it, they yipped. They were totally ignoring the big problem of Mom being up in a tree, and concentrating on the minor little thing of the "y'knows." It was enough to make a person bite bugs.

"Forget it," she snarled, storming out of the house. She heard the twins put down their equipment and follow her, so maybe they weren't altogether hopeless.

She went to stand under the tree with Katie and her friends. "Mom?" she called, looking upward.

"Yes?" Mom leaned over to peer down at her.

Marybeth wondered what she should say. If Mom had really flipped out or something, she might fall from the tree if Marybeth said too much. She might not even realize she was *in* a tree.

Marybeth cleared her throat. "Is it okay if I have the Bee Theres over for a meeting this afternoon?" That seemed like a safe thing to say.

"Sure, honey," Mom said from her perch on the Limbo Limb. "You can have them over any time you want. You know that."

"Hi-yi, Mom," Garth said, waving at her with a grin, and Grant said, "Hi." He was grinning too. "Whatcha doing up there?"

"Hi, yourselves," Mom said. "Did you find the waffles I left in the oven to keep warm for you?"

She wasn't answering Garth's question.

"Sure, Mom, we found them," Grant said. "You know us. If there's food anywhere, we can sniff it out."

They were acting as if it were perfectly normal for a mother to sit high in a tree right in the front yard where anyone could see her. Sometimes Marybeth wondered if boys had any sense at all.

"We're going to talk about going to girls camp at

our meeting," she said, careful not to include any "y'knows" that the twins could yip about. "It'll be at Cougar Lake in August. We're going to look around for ways to earn the money for it."

"There's a snake at Cougar Lake Camp," Garth said.

"Name's Norman," Grant added.

"He's big," Garth said. "Real big."

Grant nodded. "Seven feet long. Maybe eight. Mean."

"Smart, too," Garth said. "Knows how to crawl right into the lodges and curl up in a slee-heeping bag."

"That's enough," Mom said. "If the Scouts can survive Norman, the girls can too."

Far from being scared by Norman, which is what the twins intended her to be, Marybeth was happy to learn about him. She wasn't afraid of snakes, but she could use Norman as the excuse why she wasn't going to girls camp. That way she wouldn't have to tell anybody the real reason.

She faked a shiver. "I'm for sure not going any-place where there might be an eight-foot-long snake in my sleeping bag."

"I think I was wrong," Garth said. "Actually, Norman's as long as a garden hose. He can stretch almost around the whole camp."

7

"Cut it out, guys," Mom said from up in the tree. "Of course you're going to camp, Marybeth."

This was really goofy, standing there under the tree looking up at Mom, who was conversing as easily as if they were all sitting around in the family room.

"I really don't care about going to camp," Marybeth said. "I don't like camping. I hate tents."

"You always enjoyed it when you were younger," Mom said, "when we had our family campouts. Girls camp is even more fun, and you won't be in tents, anyway. You'll be in perfectly fine buildings there at Cougar Lake, and I doubt if Norman can get inside any of them."

Marybeth shook her head. "I don't want to go anyway."

"We'll talk about it when I come down."

That gave Marybeth the chance to ask what she really wanted to know. "When will that be, Mom? When are you going to come down?"

"In a little while."

Why had she gone up there? To get closer to the sun? To spy on the neighborhood kids? To carve her name in the bark of the tree?

Katie and her friends were still staring upward. "I wish *my* mom could climb trees," whispered a small red-haired boy.

Maybe a little sympathy would bring some information. Marybeth bent her head back so her voice would carry up into the tree. "I used to go up to the Limbo Limb a lot when I, y'know, had a problem," she said nervously. "Sometimes it's, y'know, a good place to go when you need to think." But what problem did Mom need to think about?

"Yip, yip," Grant said, reminding her of the "y'knows."

She ignored him. She was trying to figure out how she could get Mom to come down right now, before the Bee Theres arrived. She was worried about her, and besides, it would be terminally embarrassing to Marybeth if they came and saw Mom up there.

It would be almost as embarrassing as having them find out the real reason why Marybeth didn't want to go to camp.

CHAPTER
2

It was too late. There was no way Marybeth could prevent the other Bee Theres from seeing Mom up there in the tree. They were coming down the street that very moment. Even if she ran toward them and herded them in through the back door by way of the backyard, they were going to spot Mom perched up there on the Limbo Limb like an oversize canary in her bright yellow jogging outfit.

She'd never done anything like this before. She'd always been a perfect mom-type mom, the kind who was there when the kids came home from school. The kind who made lunches on school mornings and went to PTA meetings and baked cookies for homeroom parties.

She was not the kind who did embarrassing stuff like take the part of the berserk Relief Society president in the roadshow, as Sunshine's mother had done. Sunshine hadn't seemed to mind that her mom skipped around the stage like a teenager, but Marybeth had been glad her own mother had sat in the audience the way mothers were supposed to do.

Mom definitely wasn't the kind to climb trees.

There had to be something wrong, and now that the Bee Theres had arrived, Marybeth wished she'd told Carlie over the phone that she wasn't going to camp. That way the Bee Theres wouldn't have come to her house to talk about it.

She was sure they'd already spotted Mom up there, what with Katie and her friends, as well as Garth and Grant, all gaping upward with their mouths open.

She was right. While the girls were still half a block away, Sunshine called, "Whatcha doing up in the tree, Sister Stewart? Feeding birds?"

Marybeth's mother waved. "Hi, girls," she said.

She didn't answer Sunshine's question.

Sunshine repeated it to Marybeth as she and the other Bee Theres came to stand under the tree. "What's your mom doing up in the tree?" She whispered it this time, as if she didn't want Marybeth's mother to hear. You could tell she too thought that something was seriously wrong.

The Bee Theres stared upward along with everybody else. They looked like a nest of giant baby birds standing there with their mouths gaping open.

Up in the tree, Mom gazed silently down at them. There was a small smile on her face.

Marybeth suddenly had a horrifying new thought. What if Mom started dropping stuff down into those open mouths? What if she had some kind of fixation about being a monstrous mother bird, sitting up there, and got the idea she should feed all those babies below?

But all Mom did was say, "Marybeth tells me you're going to be scouting around today for ways to earn money for girls camp."

The other four Bee Theres nodded solemnly.

"Good," Mom said from the tree. "If you're going to be looking around the neighborhood, would you like to do some Ding-Dong Ditching? I made some cookies this morning and packaged them up."

Ding-Dong Ditching was Marybeth's mom's way of keeping both the elderly single people of the neighborhood and the kids entertained one afternoon each month. She'd bake up lots of cookies and stack them on paper plates with plastic wrap around them. Then she'd send a couple of her kids and their friends around to the houses in the neighborhood where elderly people lived alone. They would ring the doorbell, ditch the cookies on the porch, then run away. The people knew who made the cookies and who left them, and the kids knew they knew, but it was fun anyway.

"Sure, we could do that, Sister Stewart," Becca said carefully, and the others nodded, looking at one another, then up into the tree again.

Marybeth felt she was going to die right there on the spot from a mixture of worry and embarrassment. Maybe dying was the easiest way out. Then she wouldn't have to convince the others that she couldn't go to girls camp. She wouldn't ever have to tell them the real reason why and see their eyes slide away and hear them snicker behind their hands. She wouldn't have to watch them whisper to others that Marybeth . . . that Marybeth . . .

She waited to drop dead.

But she didn't.

Instead, looking up at Mom, she had a brilliant idea. She wouldn't have to tell the Bee Theres the real reason why she wasn't going. They could see with their own eyes that something had happened to Mom. Marybeth could just say she couldn't leave home while Mom was suffering from whatever she was suffering from. That was a better excuse than the snake, Norman.

Of course, using Mom as an excuse didn't change the fact that Marybeth was very worried about what her affliction was. But Dad would be able to fix her up, since he worked with people with problems all the time. And in the meantime, Marybeth might as well make use of the opportunity.

"Let's go," she said to the other Bee Theres.

Leaving Garth and Grant and Katie and her friends baby-birding it under the tree, they headed toward the kitchen to get Mom's neat packages of cookies.

"Is it okay to go away and leave her up there?" Becca twitched her head toward Marybeth's mother in the tree.

"I think so." Marybeth glanced back. She hoped the other Bee Theres noticed how worried she was. "Garth and Grant will watch her."

To make sure of that, she went back to them and said, "Will you guys, y'know, keep an eye on her?"

"Yip," Garth said, reminding her of the "y'know."

"We might even get up there *with* her," Grant said.

They probably would. They were goofy enough to haul up some food and have a whole party up there.

Sighing, Marybeth returned to the Bee Theres and led them to the kitchen.

The cookies were lemon bars this time, since the lemon tree was heavy with fruit. Mom didn't like anything to go to waste.

Each plate was identified with a small card. One

read "Miss Blake" and another one read "Mrs. Yost," who lived next door. There was also a card for Brother Turvey, who was a member of the church. A fourth plate had a card that read "For the Bee Theres, when you get hungry."

"Let's eat them now," Carlie said.

Carlie was the smallest of the Bee Theres, and also the hungriest. When they had their really serious club meetings at McDonald's, their favorite place to eat, Carlie could put away a Big Mac, large fries, and a giant chocolate shake and still want more.

"Let's keep them until we're through looking for ways to earn money for camp," Elena suggested. "That way, if we don't find anything, they can be our consolation."

"Vote," Marybeth said. The Bee Theres didn't have any club officers, but she was the Beehive class president, so it was her place to settle things like this. "All in favor of eating the cookies right now, please signify, y'know, by raising your right hand."

Carlie giggled as she raised her hand. "You sound just like Bishop Talbot when he's sustaining people in church."

"All in favor of later?" Marybeth asked.

Elena, Sunshine, and Becca raised their hands.

"Save," Marybeth said. "They'll, y'know, give us something to look forward to."

"We have plenty to look forward to," Carlie grumbled as they each picked up a plate of cookies and went out the back door to go across the lots to Mrs. Yost's house. "What with girls camp and all," she finished.

"*If* we get to go," Elena said. "Remember, we have to earn one hundred dollars for each one of us."

Sunshine nodded. "That's a lot of money. That's five hundred dollars that our class has to earn."

"Just four hundred," Marybeth said sadly.

Sunshine looked at her. "You get a D in math, Marybeth. There are five of us, at one hundred dollars each. That adds up to five hundred dollars."

Marybeth let her face lengthen mournfully. "I can't go."

They all stopped to stare at her. "Can't go?" They looked as shocked as if she'd said she'd just taken up smoking or something.

Marybeth motioned back toward her house and the big tree in the front yard where her mother sat. "How can I go away and leave Mom when she's, y'know, like that?"

They all looked toward the big tree, then back at Marybeth.

"She's all right," Sunshine said. "My mom always does stuff like that."

16

"That's the point," Marybeth replied. "My mom *doesn't.*"

"But your dad will take care of her." Elena's face looked earnest but unconvincing.

"Marybeth," Becca wailed, "you *have* to go. It wouldn't be the same without you."

"Moms do strange things when they start getting old," Carlie commented. "My mom opens the refrigerator door, then forgets what she opened it for."

"They all, y'know, do that," Marybeth said. "My mom's done that for years."

They were at Mrs. Yost's front door by now. They ditched the cookies, ding-donged the doorbell, and ran off to hide behind the shrubbery in her front yard.

"Maybe we could sell cookies to make some money," Sunshine suggested.

Marybeth shook her head. "Darla says the Laurels are planning to take orders for peach pie and lasagna and stuff like that to raise their money. They'd be mad if we horned in on their business."

Darla was her older sister, and she was as good a cook as their mom was. Her lasagna and peach pie were fabulous.

Becca's eyes brightened. "Let *Darla* stay home with your mom. She's been to girls camp before. She won't mind staying home."

"This is, y'know, her last year," Marybeth said. "She wants to go. I'll have other years to go." Or maybe she wouldn't *ever* go, Marybeth thought sadly. Very likely the reason she didn't want to go would be just as strong next summer as it was this year.

"Well," Becca said, "you can't stay home from girls camp just because your mother sits up in a tree."

"There are other reasons why I'm not going," Marybeth said hastily.

Sunshine narrowed her eyes. "You mean like you wet the bed or something?"

Marybeth put on a look of indignation. "I was with all of you at the old historical farm. Did I, y'know, wet the bed there?"

"No," admitted Sunshine. "Then what? What other reason?"

"There's a snake at girls camp." Marybeth could feel her face getting red. She felt flustered. She hadn't really meant to mention the snake. She wished she'd simply stuck to the mother-in-the-tree story without bringing up anything else.

"Norman," Becca said. "Everybody knows about Norman. He's just a legend, Marybeth. Somebody made him up."

"I hate snakes," Marybeth said weakly.

Sunshine looked surprised. "Since when?"

18

"Shhh," Elena cautioned, pointing at Mrs. Yost's house.

They watched Mrs. Yost open her door, pick up the plate, and sniff at the cookies. "Tell Mrs. Stewart thanks," she called, then went back inside.

"I guess it's not much of a secret as to who bakes the cookies," Elena commented.

"Secrets are hard to keep," Carlie said.

Marybeth agreed, but there was one secret she was for sure going to keep.

They went on to Miss Blake's house and left a plate of cookies on her front porch. Becca eyed the overgrown yard as they hurried back down the walk. "Maybe we could earn money by doing yard work."

Carlie shook her head. "Gregory says the Scouts plan to earn money for camp by cleaning yards."

She blushed when she said it. That was because she liked Gregory a lot. He wasn't a member of the church, but he had started coming to their ward because he lived next door to Sister Rhoda Jackson, their Beehive teacher, and she had been getting him involved with the activities. He also seemed to like Carlie as much as she liked him.

Well, if the Scouts were going to earn money by cleaning yards and the Laurels were going to cook for people, what else was there? Marybeth felt a little more cheerful. Maybe they wouldn't find any way to make the necessary money for girls camp. Then her problem would solve itself.

But the thought had no sooner crossed her mind than Sunshine pointed across the street at Brother Turvey's house.

"Look," she said. "Look at all that neat stuff he's lugging out to the curb. *That's* what we can do."

Brother Turvey was carrying a couple of wooden chairs toward the curb where there was a pile of other stuff, including a tall lamp and an old chest of drawers.

"You mean help him get rid of his trash?" Becca asked.

"No, dumb-dumb." Sunshine was practically jumping up and down. "We'll have a garage sale. Let's go over and ask if we can have all that stuff he's getting rid of. We can *sell* it."

She ran across the street and was already talking to him when the other Bee Theres arrived.

"He says we can have it," Sunshine rejoiced.

"Take whatever you want," Brother Turvey said. "I was putting it out for Super Trash day. Want to get rid of it all. Going to move to an apartment now that the wife's gone."

Sister Turvey had died the year before. Marybeth had liked her a lot because she always seemed interested in what the young people were doing.

"We're trying to, y'know, raise money for girls camp," Marybeth told Brother Turvey. "This will give us a start." Not much of a start, she thought happily. The old stuff there at the curb wouldn't bring in anywhere near one hundred dollars, let alone five hundred dollars. She could even be totally noble and say whatever money they could raise could go to pay for the others since she wasn't going anyway.

"Lots more where this came from." Brother Turvey waved his arm toward his house. "Attic's full. You can have anything up there. Go on up and see what you can use."

"Yay!" yelled Elena and Carlie and Sunshine and Becca. Grabbing Marybeth's hand, they headed for Brother Turvey's house. "No," Marybeth said almost in a whisper. "I don't want to go up to the attic. I don't care what's up there."

But she was carried along by the others, in through the kitchen, down the hallway, and up the narrow stairs.

It was stifling hot on the stairs, but that wasn't what made Marybeth's heart pound so hard she could scarcely breath. Looking ahead toward the dark, shadowed attic, she wished desperately that she could get away and run back down the stairs to the bright daylight outside.

CHAPTER
3

"Wait," Marybeth gasped. "I have to stop for a minute."

"You can't be tired already, Marybeth." Becca was behind her on the stairway. "Here, I'll push."

Marybeth stared at the darkness at the top of the stairs. "It's okay, Becca. I'll just wait here while the rest of you go look in the attic."

But Becca didn't stop pushing. "We need you. Let's go."

Marybeth pulled in a deep breath of air, trying to calm herself. She looked down at her feet rather than into the blackness at the top of the stairs.

But it didn't help. Her heart pounded even faster.

She took another deep breath and began to cough.

"Oh, oh," she gasped, "the dust is, y'know, getting

to me. I guess I'll have to go back downstairs while the rest of you, y'know, look at the stuff."

She turned to go, but Becca blocked her way.

"We haven't even stirred up any dust yet," Becca said. "Go on, Marybeth. You'll be all right."

Again she pushed Marybeth toward the attic.

Marybeth tried closing her eyes, but that didn't help. She knew what was up there in the attic. Darkness.

She was totally terrified, petrified, horrified of the dark. She couldn't go into the dismal, dark attic.

Marybeth had been afraid of the dark ever since the Bee Theres had spent two weeks at an old historical farm in Utah where there were no bright street lights. Not even house lights, since everything at the old farm was as it had been in 1917, before electricity had come to the rural areas. There'd been only dim, flickering lamplight, and phantom shadows, and, worst of all, the GHOST that had appeared in the total darkness.

Sunshine, Elena, and Carlie were in the attic now.

"Turn on the light up there," Marybeth squeaked, almost unable to talk. "I can't see."

The attic must have a light. How else could they see what was there?

"I can't find a switch," said Sunshine.

"Maybe it's one of those hang-down lights with a

pull-chain," Elena said. "You'll have to walk in a ways and swing your arms around over your head to find it."

The thought of going into a dark attic and swinging her arms around made Marybeth sweat. What if there were spider webs with dead flies caught in them? What if there were huge, fat spiders? What if there were *ghosts*?

She shivered, shrinking back against the wall of the stairwell.

A light went on, but it was dim, even dimmer than the one on the stairs. As dim as those flickering kerosene lamps at the old historical farm.

She *couldn't* go into that attic.

"Move it, Marybeth." Becca puffed a little as she continued to push her. "Let's see what kind of treasures we've got here."

There wasn't anything to do but go on. Marybeth couldn't tell the Bee Theres, or anybody else for that matter, how she was terrified of the dark. They'd laugh. They'd tease. They'd make fun of a twelve-year-old baby who was afraid of the dark. Would they kick her out of the Bee Theres for being a mega-wimp? Would they even throw her out of the Beehive class?

"Okay, okay," she said, forcing herself to take those last few steps and enter the cluttered, dark attic.

There were no windows. No outside light at all. If that fading lightbulb that hung from the ceiling went out, they'd be in almost total darkness, except for the dim light from the stairwell.

"Hey, look at all the neat stuff," Carlie said. "Maybe we won't even have to find any more things for our garage sale." She picked up a book from a three-foot-high stack that rose from the floor.

Choking back her fear, Marybeth looked around. An old ironing board stood on three spidery legs beside her. A child's painted wooden chair hung from a rafter, draped with cobwebs. There was a cardboard box marked "Summer dresses," and another one that said "Baby clothes."

"I'll, y'know, run back downstairs," she said quickly, "and, y'know, ask Brother Turvey if his kids don't, y'know, want some of this stuff. Y'know, the baby clothes, and the, y'know, books and things, y'know."

It was a good thing Garth wasn't there to yip every time she said "y'know." He'd need a dog license, what with all the "y'knows" she had just let loose.

Becca shook her head. "He said we could have everything up here. We'll ask him when we all go back downstairs."

She looked at Marybeth with narrowed eyes.

Did she guess Marybeth's secret? Was she going to tell the others that she was terrified of the dark?

Quickly Marybeth said, "Look at the old trunks in the corner." She headed toward the darkest part of the attic, where two ancient trunks stood side by side. "Let's, y'know, see what's in them."

Her heart rattling in her chest, she forced herself to walk over to the trunks. The others followed.

"Wow," Sunshine gasped, "I wonder what's in them."

"Money, maybe," Carlie suggested.

Marybeth put out a hand to raise the lid of the first trunk. If she touched a spider, she'd faint on the spot.

"Maybe," Becca said in a whisper, "it's full of skeletons!" It took all of Marybeth's willpower not to whip her hand back from the trunk. But she managed to say, "Silly!" and open the lid.

Something white rose from the trunk, and all of the girls screamed and stepped back.

All except Marybeth. She stayed where she was, frozen to the spot with fear. She was absolutely paralyzed. It was like Ruby's ghost at the old farm all over again.

Sunshine stepped slowly forward. She laughed. "It's just a white dress," she said, sounding relieved.

"It's caught on something on the lid, and that's what pulled it up."

She reached out to unhook the dress and hold it up so they could all see.

Now the other Bee Theres came back to look.

"I guess Marybeth is the only one of us with any courage." Carlie looked admiringly at her. "She didn't even flinch."

"Hey, I want you in my cabin at girls camp," Elena said. "I'll need somebody with a little courage out there in those dark pine woods with the bears and coyotes."

"Don't forget the bats," Becca put in. "Watch out for Dracula."

"And that snake, Norman," Sunshine said. "Good old Norman will be there to greet us."

They all laughed together. Except for Marybeth. She was still paralyzed.

She managed a grin and a modest look in response to the praise for her "courage." If they only knew!

There was absolutely no way in the world that she could survive a week at girls camp. Dark woods? Coyotes? Bats? No way!

But now was not the time to bring up that subject again.

She took a deep breath and looked closely at the white dress Sunshine was holding up.

"It's a wedding dress," she said, her voice sounding thin and flat to her own ears. "Look at all the, y'know, lace."

As the other Bee Theres ooohed and aaaahed, she pried her stiff fingers loose from the lid of the trunk, leaning it back against a rafter where the roof slanted down to meet the floor. Taking care not to stagger, she walked shakily to an old wicker rocking chair that stood close by and collapsed in it.

"Why don't you model the dress, Sunshine?" Now her voice sounded hoarse. "It looks like just about your size."

Looking pleased by the suggestion, Sunshine maneuvered to pull the dress on over her shorts and shirt.

Becca stopped her. "Hey, dumb-dumb, how's that going to look? Go over there in the dark and take off your other clothes so the dress will fit nice."

"Since when are we all so modest?" Sunshine asked, but she headed for the dark corner.

While she was gone, Carlie leaned over the old trunk. "Let's see what else is here." Her arms disappeared down into the depths of the trunk, and she brought up something wrapped in a blanket of some kind. "It feels like . . . "

"Like what?" demanded Becca. "Unwrap it, Carlie."

Carlie folded back the blanket. "Like a fiddle," she said.

She held up a violin, darkened by age.

"Oh, my," whispered Elena. She reached out to touch the violin. "Oh, my."

Elena was the musician of the group. She had a beautiful singing voice, and she could play almost any instrument.

"Oh, my," she said. "If we sold this, I'll bet we'd have enough money to pay for camp for almost all of the Young Women in the ward."

Marybeth's heart sank. She'd been hoping that there wouldn't be enough stuff to make a garage sale worthwhile. She'd been hoping that if there *was* enough stuff, there would be only enough to pay for camp for four of them. Then she could volunteer to be the one to stay home.

The wood of the violin glowed in the dim light from the overhead bulb. It looked expensive.

"We'll *have* to ask Brother Turvey about that," Marybeth said. "I don't think he, y'know, really meant we could have *everything* up here."

"Maybe you're right." Elena stroked the wood of the violin gently. "I wonder who used to play it."

Sunshine, in the white dress, glided over to touch the instrument.

Marybeth's heart lurched because in the gloomy attic Sunshine looked almost identical to Ruby's ghost, complete with the long braid down her back.

"I think we'd better ask Brother Turvey about this dress too," she said. "If it was Sister Turvey's wedding dress, he wouldn't want us to be selling it at a garage sale, would he?"

"But he *said*," Becca objected.

Marybeth stood up, her legs still shaking just a little. "But he also said he didn't know what was up here. We have to ask."

"I was hoping our camp money problems would be solved," Becca grumbled. "If we give up *everything*, we'll have to start all over again."

That was all right with Marybeth.

Downstairs, Brother Turvey's eyes filled with tears when he saw Sunshine in the white dress.

He set down the box he'd been carrying from the curb back to his garage. "That was my Pearl's wedding dress," he said softly. Marybeth knew for sure they wouldn't be selling the dress at their garage sale.

Brother Turvey fished a red bandanna from his pocket and wiped it across his face. "Most beautiful angel I ever saw, Pearl was in that dress. Never forget how she looked in the temple that morning when we got married."

He blew his nose into the bandanna, then stuffed it back into his pocket.

"You girls don't mind if I keep it, do you?" he asked.

Elena held up the violin. "Here's something else you'll want to keep."

He came over and touched it, and there was remembering in his eyes. "Pearl used to play that when we first got married. Put it away when the kids started coming. Always meant to get back to it. Never did."

Silently Elena handed the violin to him.

Marybeth, breathing more calmly now that they were back in the sunlight, had an inspiration. "Brother Turvey," she said, "there are, y'know, a lot of things there in the attic that might be valuable. Maybe you'd like to sell them yourself. They could bring in a lot of money."

Brother Turvey was still lightly stroking the violin. "Well, sure could use *that*," he said. "But I don't know how to tell how much any of it is worth."

"Sister Jackson would know," Marybeth said.

Sister Jackson was their Beehive class leader, and she knew everything.

"We can ask her to, y'know, come over and pick

31

out the good stuff that you can sell to, y'know, an antique shop or something. Then we'll take the rest for our garage sale." Marybeth tried to not see the glare that Becca gave her. She was giving back all the things that would bring in the five hundred dollars they needed for camp.

"That would be right nice," Brother Turvey said.

After Sunshine changed back into her own clothes and hung the wedding dress carefully in Brother Turvey's bedroom, the Bee Theres helped him carry all the curb stuff back to the garage. There was still a lot, but not five hundred dollars' worth, Marybeth noted with satisfaction.

So, if Mom continued to suffer from whatever it was that made her get up into the tree, Marybeth would have enough excuses not to go to girls camp.

Mom was still up in the tree when the Bee Theres got back to Marybeth's house. Not only was she there, but she was also just finishing tying a lawn chair to the Limbo Limb, which had a handy crook in it just perfect to lean the back of the chair against, with its legs over the limb.

So what was she planning to do, stay up there forever?

What was wrong with her, anyway?

CHAPTER
4

This time Marybeth and the other Bee Theres didn't stand underneath the tree and stare up at her mother. Instead Marybeth whispered, "Act casual," then said, "Hi, Mom."

Taking her cue, the others said "Hi, Sister Stewart," as if seeing a mother tying a lawn chair to a limb high in a tree was something that happened every day of the week.

The other kids—Katie and her friends and Garth and Grant—had gone somewhere else, probably to the backyard because Marybeth could hear laughter and the whump-whump of the trampoline.

"We'll be in my room, Mom," Marybeth called. "We'll be talking, y'know, about girls camp." She stared up at her mother, trying to see if she looked flushed or had a strange rash or something that

33

would give a clue about her behavior. But she appeared perfectly normal, except that she was in a tree.

"Okay." Mom had finished tying the lawn chair to the limb now and sat down slowly in it, as if testing it out. "Did you do all the Ding-Dong Ditching?"

"All but our own plate," Marybeth called. "We're going to, y'know, take care of that when we get to my room."

"Right," Mom said.

Marybeth waited for more, but her mother didn't say anything further.

"Mom?" Marybeth craned her neck upward. "We've decided how we're going to make money for camp."

"Good," Mom said. "I'll be anxious to hear."

"I'll tell you when you come down." Marybeth waited again.

Mom didn't say anything.

"When are you, y'know, coming down?"

"Later," Mom said.

She picked something off the limb beside her and looked down at her lap. She seemed to be either reading or writing, the way she'd done earlier. Was it a journal she was writing in?

"We're going in now," Marybeth called.

"Fine, honey. 'Bye." Mom waved, and Marybeth

thought she saw a pencil in her hand. Or it could have been a knitting needle.

She led the other Bee Theres into the house.

"What do you think is the matter with her?" Sunshine whispered, twitching her head back toward the tree.

"I don't know. I'm really worried." Marybeth glanced back at her mother.

"Don't worry about it," Sunshine soothed. "Moms do really weird things sometimes. My mom had a Habakkuk Dig-In last week."

"A what?" Marybeth asked.

"Habakkuk Dig-In. You know, the book in the Bible between Nahum and Zephaniah." Sunshine hummed a little bit of a song they'd learned back in Primary that helped them memorize the books of the Bible. "She said she'd never learned much about that book, so she invited some friends over one night for a Habakkuk Dig-In."

"That *is* weird." Elena looked puzzled. "What did they do?"

"They sat around and read the whole book—it's only three chapters," Sunshine said. "Then they talked about it."

That sounded very typical of Sunshine's mother, Marybeth thought. She was always doing strange

35

stuff. But the thing was, her own mother *didn't* do that kind of thing. Not normally.

"*My* mom watches soap operas while she works on her computer," Carlie offered.

"Mine likes to poke around old cemeteries looking for names of relatives to put on her family history sheets," Becca said. "When she finds relatives, she stands there and talks to them."

She paused, letting that sink in. Then, shaking her head, she said, "But she doesn't sit up in trees."

The other Bee Theres gazed sympathetically at Marybeth.

"We'll be there for you if you need us," Carlie reminded her.

That's what the Bee Theres Club was all about. The five girls had made a vow to be there for each other when needed.

Marybeth was glad they'd got back to the major problem of *her* mom. Inwardly she rejoiced that the others had been there to witness the scene that had just been played outside. If the garage sale thing was successful, she might have to fall back totally on the excuse that she couldn't go to camp because she had to take care of her mother. After the experience she'd just had in the attic, she knew she couldn't possibly go. If she was forced to go, there was no telling what might happen. She might even have a heart attack from fright in that dark mountain place, like the one she'd almost had in the attic when that white dress rose up out of the old trunk.

Marybeth's older sister Darla stuck her head around the kitchen door as the Bee Theres came in. "Oh," she said, "I thought you might be Mom. What's the scoop on her, anyway? How come she's in the tree?"

"I don't know," Marybeth said.

Why was Darla asking her? Darla was the smart one. She was seventeen and would be leaving for BYU in a few more weeks. She ought to know more about Mom's problem than Marybeth did.

Darla shrugged as if it was no big deal. "Well, she'll be down later to fix dinner." She waved a thick envelope. "Randy's mission call came in the mail today."

Randy was their older brother. He'd just turned nineteen in June and had submitted his mission papers to church headquarters in Salt Lake City.

All of the Bee Theres squealed and ran to cluster around Darla.

"Where's he going?" Carlie asked.

"Does he know his call came?" Becca asked.

"Does Mom know?" Marybeth asked.

Darla held the envelope over her head so the girls couldn't touch it. "First question, I don't know where he's going," she said. "He'll open his letter when he gets home from work. Second question, no. Third question, yes, Mom knows. I told her as soon as I got home and looked at the mail."

"What did she say?" Marybeth asked.

"She was excited. Said she'd be down by the time Randy gets home from work." Darla walked over and parked the fat envelope on the mantel.

Marybeth was relieved. If Mom *hadn't* reacted to something as important as a mission call, Marybeth would have been truly worried. Randy would be going away somewhere for two years, maybe to Russia or Brazil or Hong Kong or maybe even Montana, to tell people about the church. Two years! Of course she'd come down.

But she'd tied that lawn chair up there on the limb, so that meant she planned to go back up there, didn't it? Marybeth could still use her as an excuse for not going to camp.

She could use Randy too, she realized suddenly. He'd probably be leaving for the Missionary Training Center in Provo at just about the same time as the girls would be going to camp. She couldn't be expected to leave at a time like that, not when he'd probably be having his missionary farewell at church, and then they'd be seeing him off, or maybe they'd all drive him to Provo. She couldn't miss that.

No, there was no question about it. Marybeth would have to stay home. She was safe. She could join in with the other Bee Theres in the fund raising, since, after all, she wanted to be a good sport. But then, when the others left for girls camp, she of course wouldn't be able to go.

"Let's go upstairs," she said happily. "We need to make that call to Sister Jackson."

"And eat the cookies." Carlie picked up the plate of lemon squares Marybeth's mother had made for them.

Up in her room, Marybeth punched in Sister Jackson's phone number while the other Bee Theres munched the lemon squares.

"Your mom still makes the best cookies," Carlie said, as if that meant she'd *have* to be okay if she could still do something that well. "Maybe she's writing recipes up there in the tree."

But why would she get up in the tree to do that? Why would she get up there to do anything?

Sister Jackson answered her phone, and Marybeth explained to her about how Brother Turvey said they could have the stuff from his attic for a garage sale to raise money for camp but how they thought some of the things were too valuable for him just to give away.

"Some of them might be antiques," she said. "Can you come over and, y'know, tell us what you think?"

"I'll be glad to," Sister Jackson said. "I'm proud of you girls doing what you think is best for him."

"There'll, y'know, be a few things left over for a garage sale," Marybeth said.

"What clever girls you are to think of a garage sale," Sister Jackson said. "We'll put a notice in the Sunday bulletin that we're looking for donations. We might even make enough money to pay for our total camp cost."

"That's what we thought. Can you meet us at—" Marybeth almost said "—at Brother Turvey's house," but she changed that instead to "Can you meet us at, y'know, my house?" She wanted Sister Jackson to see Mom up there in the tree. Otherwise she might not accept that excuse for Marybeth staying home from camp. Maybe she would even know what was wrong with Mom. She knew so many things.

"Yes, I can meet you there," Sister Jackson said. "It will take me about ten minutes."

Marybeth hung up and took the last lemon square on the plate. "She'll be right over."

She'd just munched down on the cookie when Darla knocked at her bedroom door and came in. She held another envelope, a small, pale peach-colored one this time. "I was so excited about Randy's mission call," she said, "that I forget to tell you there's a letter for the Bee Theres."

"Oh, wow." Sunshine leaped up from her place on Marybeth's bed and reached for the letter.

Darla sneezed as she handed it to Sunshine. Darla was allergic to almost everything, and there was probably perfume on that pretty envelope that made her sneeze, Marybeth decided.

"I think I'm allergic to Beehives," Darla said as she left the room. "See you later."

Sunshine looked at the letter. "It's from Pamela!" she exclaimed.

Wasn't it just like Pamela to send a pale peach, perfumed letter!

Pamela had been their Beehive teacher before Sister Jackson. Pamela had been the most exciting person they'd ever known. She'd never made them call her "Sister Spencer," so she was more like one of them than a teacher. She'd been an airline attendant who flew all around the world. But she'd gone home to Idaho to get ready for her wedding, which would be quite soon now.

Sister Jackson was okay as a teacher, but Pamela! Could it be that she was writing to say she was coming back? Would she take over the class again?

"Open it," Marybeth and Elena said in unison.

Quickly Sunshine pried up the flap on the back and took out the sheets of paper. She began reading.

"Read it aloud!" demanded Becca.

41

Sunshine cleared her throat. *"Dear Becca, Carlie, Elena, Marybeth, and Sunshine,"* she read. *"I'm addressing you in alphabetical order so that you'll know I love each of you equally. I miss my little Bees so much. I hope you haven't forgotten me."*

Sunshine looked up. "Huh! Who could ever forget Pamela."

"Read," the other girls chorused.

"As you know, I'll be coming back to California soon for my wedding. Steve and I will be married in the Los Angeles Temple, and we'll be having the reception in the cultural hall there at the ward. What I want to ask is, will the five of you be my bridesmaids at the reception?"

Sunshine squealed and fell on the bed.

"Does it really say that?" Marybeth snatched the letter from Sunshine. Her eyes skimmed the paper, and she collapsed beside Sunshine. "It does! It really says that! Oh, wow! Bridesmaids!"

Squealing, Becca, Carlie, and Elena crowded close to look at the letter as if they had to see the words with their own eyes.

Carlie plucked the sheets of paper from Marybeth's hand. *"If you say yes,"* she read, *"I'll need your opinions on the dresses."*

"Our opinions!" Becca said. "Eeeek, I can't believe it!"

Nobody ever asked for *their* opinions.

Carlie went on reading the letter. *"I want you girls to be happy with your bridesmaids' dresses, so why don't you give me a suggestion as to what color you all like?"*

"The wedding," Marybeth said. "When is it?" She crossed her fingers, hoping it would be in August. During the week of girls camp in August. Or maybe the week before so they'd have to be there in town for the dress fittings and everything.

Carlie read swiftly down the page. "September seventeenth," she said. "Oh good, that will give us plenty of time to get ready after we get home from camp."

Oh well. It didn't matter. Marybeth had sufficient excuses not to go already. She glanced out of the window at the tree in front.

Her mother wasn't there any longer. She must have come down out of the tree. And Sister Jackson hadn't arrived in time to see her sitting up there.

"What do you think, Marybeth?" Sunshine said.

She hadn't been listening. What were they asking about? The bridemaids' dresses? The garage sale? Something about camp?

She cleared her throat. "What do the rest of you think?"

"We think it's a McDonald's problem," Sunshine said.

Whenever the Bee Theres had something major

to discuss, they went to McDonald's and munched Big Macs and fries while they talked.

"I think so too," Marybeth said. She checked the tree again, but her mother didn't suddenly reappear there on her chair. Momentarily worried, Marybeth walked in what she hoped was a nonchalant way to the window to see if Mom had fallen out or something. Perhaps she was lying on the ground, all hurt and bleeding.

But her mother was nowhere in sight.

As Marybeth stood there by the window, Sister Jackson drove up in her car.

"Let's go to McDonald's for lunch tomorrow to discuss it," Marybeth said. Whatever the problem was that Sunshine and the others had in mind, she'd find out when they got to the Golden Arches. "Sister Jackson's here."

Carlie shoved Pamela's letter into a pocket of her jeans, and the Bee Theres went downstairs together.

Marybeth's mother was in the living room. She stood by the fireplace mantel, holding Randy's letter and looking like her old self. You'd never have guessed she'd just been sitting up in the tree.

"Hi, girls," she said to the Bee Theres. "I guess you know Randy got his mission call."

They nodded.

"He'll probably be leaving soon after girls camp,"

Mom said. "But with stake conference coming up and three other missionaries leaving this summer, it may be that the bishop will have to schedule Randy's farewell earlier, before you girls go to camp."

Oh no. Marybeth felt like crying. Suddenly she was right back to Square One. If Mom was down out of the tree and if Randy's farewell was held before girls camp and if he wasn't leaving until after camp, then her excuses for not going had faded away.

Unless the garage sale totally failed. And there was still Norman, the snake at girls camp.

But the Bee Theres knew she wasn't afraid of snakes. Was she going to have to confess the real reason why she didn't want to go? Was she going to ha to tell them she was afraid of the dark?

CHAPTER
5

Sister Jackson was enthusiastic about the things in Brother Turvey's attic.

"The girls were right," she told him. "You've got some good antiques here. You should call an antique dealer, if you really want to sell them."

"Think I ought to? I thought it was all just old worn-out stuff. Most of it belonged to my mother. It was in the house I grew up in. I was going to give it to the girls here for a garage sale." He touched an old oak table, with a soft, faraway look on his face.

Marybeth could tell that the memories about it were good. She tried to concentrate on his face and not on where they were. In the attic. The dark, ghostly attic.

Even full of people, the dismal attic seemed scary to her. Brother Turvey had a big flashlight that he shone around, but there still were shadows and cobwebs and odd, dark shapes that she felt uneasy about. In the corner opposite where they stood was a dress form that in the murky light could be a headless ghost. A stuffed plastic bag dangled like some poor, dead thing from a nail driven into a rafter. What was in it? If it should tear, what would flutter out of it? What if the old vacuum hose that snaked across the floor close to Marybeth's feet should suddenly begin to slither around?

How much worse it would be if they were off in the dark mountains, where every tree muttered in the night and unseen creatures wailed and chittered in the darkness. And Norman, long as a garden hose, was coiled up somewhere, waiting for them.

And now she had no good excuses that she could tell the others about why she couldn't go to girls camp. Certainly she couldn't tell them the real reason—that she was afraid of the dark.

She pulled her thoughts away from that and tried to concentrate on what Sister Jackson was saying.

"This oak buffet," Sister Jackson said, touching a big piece of furniture, "it's beautiful. And look at this!" She stepped over some trash to touch another piece. "It's just like the one my grandmother had in her old farmhouse kitchen. She called it a hoosier."

She was stroking a tall cupboard that had three

little doors across the top. In the middle was a white enamel counter space, and underneath that, two wider doors. It was very nice looking.

Sister Jackson stepped back to admire it. "My grandmother kept her flour and spices and that kind of thing in the top of hers. Look." She opened the left-hand door and showed them a funnel-like thing that she said was to put flour in. "You just turn this handle and it sifts down into your mixing bowl."

The girls crowded around to look at this wonder.

Sister Jackson opened one of the wide bottom doors. "This is where you keep all your pots and pans. Brother Turvey, are you sure none of your children would want something like this?"

He shook his head. "All of them have spiffy houses with lots of carpeting and spindly chairs and shiny new furniture. All three of them told me just to get rid of all my old stuff." He looked sad as he said it.

"Why don't you use it yourself, Brother Turvey?" Marybeth asked. She didn't know why she'd said it, except she'd been visualizing Brother Turvey's house, and it seemed to her that it could be a lot cozier with some of the furniture up here rather than the chrome stuff that Sister Turvey had liked. "That, y'know, hoosier would look really great between the two big windows in your kitchen."

"It would indeed," Sister Jackson said. "And the buffet could go where those shelves with the knick-knacks are. Why, you'd have the pleasantest kitchen in seven states if you took some of this stuff down there." Her voice was beginning to sound really enthusiastic. "You could give your chrome kitchen set to the girls for their garage sale and replace it with this lovely oak table." She blew dust from the big round table and rubbed at it with a finger.

Brother Turvey's eyes brightened. "That would be nice, just like when I was a kid." Then his face drooped again. "I don't spend a lot of time in the kitchen anymore. Mostly I just microwave TV dinners."

"Well, you'd probably spend more time there if it was all cozied up with these things," Sister Jackson assured him. "Let's have somebody haul a couple of these pieces downstairs, and we'll do a little rearranging. Then I'll bake some bread in your kitchen and show you it can be like when you were a child."

Brother Turvey smiled.

Suddenly Marybeth had an idea. Sister Jackson really liked this old stuff. She was offering to bake bread for Brother Turvey. What if they should fall in love? What if they should decide to get married right away, like during the very week when the Bee Theres were supposed to go to camp? Maybe Sister Jackson would want the Bee Theres to be her bridesmaids, as Pamela did.

Then none of them could go to camp!

Brother Turvey was nodding now. "That would be right nice, Rhoda. Pearl used to bake bread. I used to make a loaf or two myself, now and then. It would be right nice if we did that sometime."

Marybeth didn't want to leave it for "sometime." If Brother Turvey and Sister Jackson were going to fall in love and get married in time to save her from going to camp, she needed to get things going *now.*

"I'll bet Quincy Adkins and some of the other guys could come over and, y'know, help us get the big things downstairs," she said. "Why don't we go call them?"

Brother Turvey looked a little doubtful. "Nobody'd be home, middle of the afternoon. All the young guys will be at work."

Marybeth shook her head. "Not Quincy. He's here to study at the acting academy, and the classes haven't started yet, and he can't find a job."

The Bee Theres had become well acquainted with Quincy when he'd been assistant director of the road-show they'd all been in. He was big and had lots of reddish blond hair, and they were all sure he'd be a famous movie star someday.

"And how about Rob Dayton?" Marybeth asked.

"He just got home from his mission and hasn't gone back to school yet."

"We'll help, too," Elena said. "It can be our service project for this month."

Sister Jackson was nodding. "Let's go call those young men. No time like the present to do this."

Brother Turvey hesitated. "Well, now, I don't know how Pearl would take to this. Never was fond of this old furniture. Was glad to put it up here when she got that kitchen set and the built-in cupboards."

"Pearl's dead," Sister Jackson reminded him gently. "Do *you* like this old furniture?"

Brother Turvey looked around. "Oh my, yes. Like I said, it's what I grew up with. My mother's kitchen was all warm and nice with that hoosier and the big table. Always had a brown pot full of flowers in the middle. And a doily. Looked homey."

"Well, then." Sister Jackson started for the stairway. "Let's get things moving."

Brother Turvey followed her. "I was thinking maybe I'd sell the house and move into a condo, now that I'm all alone," he said.

"Maybe you'll find out you'd rather stay here, once we fix up your house with all the furniture from the attic."

"Maybe so," Brother Turvey answered. "I like my

house, and I'd miss my vegetable garden if I moved into an apartment."

The Bee Theres stayed behind in the attic a few minutes longer.

"Well," Sunshine sighed gloomily, "there goes our easy way to earn camp money. I hope she doesn't decide to use *everything* up here."

Marybeth could contain herself no longer. "What if they should fall in love?" she whispered. "What if they should get married?"

"Married?" Becca asked. "But they're *old.*"

"Old people get married, too," Marybeth whispered. "Lots of them." She couldn't think of any examples. "I think she likes him."

"I think she just likes the new kitchen she's going to make for him," Sunshine commented.

"Well, maybe she'll marry him so she can live in it." Marybeth was unwilling to give up that idea. "She wants to bake bread there and make it cozy."

"My grandpa got married," Becca said in a low voice. "He said he was all ready to go on to be with my grandma after she died, but then he met this nice lady and they got married, and they go to square dances and travel all over together." As they started walking down the stairs, she added, "Maybe if Sister Jackson and Brother Turvey got married and went traveling a lot, Pamela could be our teacher again after she's married."

"We could beg her and Steve to find an apartment in our ward," Carlie said. "Then for sure she'd be our teacher again."

"But I *like* Sister Jackson," Elena protested.

"Well, so do I," Becca said. "But remember the things Pamela did with us?"

Marybeth thought of the sleep-overs and the beach parties and the shopping mall visits they used to have with Pamela. Sister Jackson was more interested in service projects, which were okay but not as exciting as the things Pamela thought of. There were a lot of reasons why Sister Jackson should marry Brother Turvey. And the sooner the better. If they'd just set the date for exactly one month from now, she thought, it would be absolutely perfect. You couldn't go to camp if your Beehive teacher was getting married, could you?

Downstairs Sister Jackson called Quincy and Rob. Neither one could come right then, but they promised to come to Brother Turvey's house the next morning.

After she hung up the phone, she turned to the Bee Theres. "If all of you can come over too, we can sort out the stuff that you can sell at your garage sale."

The Bee Theres looked at one another. They'd planned to meet at McDonald's for lunch tomorrow. Marybeth wasn't sure what the major problem was that they were going to discuss. But now, besides whatever that was, they could discuss the possibility of Sister Jackson and Brother Turvey getting married.

"Will we, y'know, be through by noon?" Marybeth asked.

Sister Jackson looked skeptical. "I doubt it. Do you have an appointment or something?"

Marybeth looked at the other Bee Theres, who all shook their heads.

"No," she said. "We can be here." They could have *dinner* at McDonald's instead of lunch.

"Fine," Sister Jackson said. "I'm inviting you all to lunch, if that's all right with Brother Turvey. We'll have newly baked bread and garden salad. . . . " She glanced out at Brother Turvey's vegetable garden in the backyard. "And I'll bring my freezer and make homemade ice cream. It'll be like when we were young." She smiled at Brother Turvey, who looked as if he'd died and gone to heaven.

Marybeth smiled, too. They must to be in love already!

That evening it seemed as if Randy would never get home. The fat letter from Salt Lake that would tell where he'd be going on his mission still sat on the mantel. It couldn't be opened until he got there.

Mom had dinner all ready and was trying to keep Garth and Grant from eating it right off the stove.

"This will be a family dinner," she kept telling them. "I want us all to sit down together after Randy opens his mission call."

Mom acted perfectly normal now. Marybeth could hardly believe she'd spent almost the whole day sitting high in the tree in the front yard.

That was both good news and bad. The good part was that she was apparently okay and hadn't flipped out, or if she had it was only temporary. The bad part was that it had been such a good excuse for Marybeth to stay home from girls camp, and now apparently it was gone.

But the lawn chair was still up in the tree. Surely that meant that Mom would be going back up there. Marybeth wasn't sure whether she hoped it did or hoped it didn't.

But now there was the possibility of something working out with Sister Jackson and Brother Turvey.

"I don't think we'll last long enough for Randy to open his mission call and everything," Grant said. "We're hungry, Ma."

Dad was standing at the stove stirring gravy. They were having Randy's favorite meal that night—fried chicken with mashed potatoes and gravy and corn on the cob. "It's good for your character to delay gratification," Dad said to Grant.

Dad was always saying stuff like that, probably because he was a psychiatrist and seemed to know what was best for everybody and how they should act. A lot of people were a little afraid of Dad because he knew so much.

But Dad was just Dad, even though he was tall and thin with silver in his black hair, which made him look like a movie star himself, even more than Quincy did. He always took off his coat when he got home, rolled up his shirt sleeves, and helped with dinner. That wasn't like any movie star Marybeth had ever heard of.

Garth and Grant groaned when he wouldn't even let them dip a piece of bread in the gravy, and he swatted their hands with the gravy spoon when they tried to steal a piece of chicken.

Marybeth wondered if anybody had told him about Mom being in the tree. Probably not. He was always telling them that he dealt with people's big problems all day and the only time he wanted to hear theirs was on weekly Gripe Night, or if it was a total emergency.

This didn't seem like an emergency, since Mom seemed so normal now. Marybeth certainly wasn't going to mention the tree. But she did wish she could manage to bring up something about what made people fall in love. Maybe Dad would have some advice on how to make sure it was going to happen to Sister Jackson and Brother Turvey.

Then suddenly Randy was home. Darla and Katie came running downstairs, and everybody went to greet him at the door, announcing in a chorus that his mission call had come and it was sitting right there on the mantel and they could hardly wait to find out where he was going.

Randy laughed and hugged everybody and then headed for the mantel in the living room, where he picked up the letter and looked at it.

"Well," he said, "this is it." He took a deep breath and put a finger under the flap of the envelope.

But before he opened it, Dad said, "Wait. Remember our tradition? Remember how we sang before Barbara and Brad opened their mission calls?"

Randy grinned. "Boy, Dad, you sure know how to torture a guy."

But he followed the rest of the family to the piano where Darla sat down on the piano bench and opened the hymn book to number 270 and played the introduction.

Marybeth gazed at her tall, great-looking brother as she began singing. *"It may not be on the mountain height or over the stormy sea,"* they all sang together. *"It may not be at the battle's front my Lord will have need of me."*

Randy was going to be such a great missionary. He'd probably convert so many people that they'd have to create a whole new stake just for them.

"But if, by a still, small voice he calls to paths that I do not know," they sang. Marybeth was going to miss Randy so much. He called her Twerp but always had time to listen to her.

The song was almost finished. *"I'll answer, dear Lord, with my hand in thine: I'll go where you want me to go."*

Anywhere but girls camp, Marybeth thought. But then she hadn't exactly received a *call* to go there.

She watched Randy open the call envelope, and was puzzled when she saw his hands tremble as he unfolded the sheaf of stiff, white papers.

CHAPTER
6

Marybeth held her breath as she watched Randy's eyes skim the writing on the front page of the papers. She kept holding it when he looked up at the circle of his family standing around him.

She finally had to breathe when he looked back at the papers again. There was a limit to how long a person could hold her breath, even on a big occasion like this.

"So where is it?" Darla was dancing around, trying to get a peek at the papers. "Where are you going?"

"I'm not sure," Randy said. He frowned a little.

Not sure! How could he be not sure? Wasn't it right there on the sheet of paper he held? Surely the people in Salt Lake had put down where he was to go on his mission. They didn't play jokes on people.

Randy made a follow-me motion and led them all

over to the world globe that stood on a small table. When they were gathered around, he spun the globe.

"Okay," he said, "now will somebody please tell me where Ecuador is?"

"Ecuador!" Mom clasped her hands together as she said it. "You'll be speaking Spanish."

Randy grinned. "Lot of good all those German classes did me."

Did that mean Randy wished he'd been called to go to Germany? Was that why his hand had trembled when he'd opened the letter from Salt Lake, because he'd been hoping to go to Germany?

Or was it something else?

Randy stopped the spinning globe. "First one to point out Ecuador can be the first one to hug me," he said.

Marybeth knew where it was. She and the other Bee Theres liked to look at the globe, especially when they played the Guy Game and got to the part where you picked the country you were going to live in with the guy you were going to marry. You would close your eyes, spin the globe, put out a finger to stop it, and wherever your finger was when the spinning stopped was where you'd live. One time when they played the Guy Game it came out that she was going to marry Joshua Becker, a guy the Bee Theres had met at the old historical farm in Utah, and they would live in Ecuador.

"Here!" She stabbed a finger at the west coast of South America, at the small orange country just south of the equator.

"Right!" Randy said. He held his arms wide, and Marybeth went into them, hugging him hard.

"Gonna miss you, Twerp," he whispered into her ear.

"I'm going to miss you too, Randy." She was just beginning to realize how *much* she'd miss him. He was going so far away. And two years was such a long time. She'd be almost fifteen when he came home. Fifteen! When he got back he'd probably be having his missionary companions come to visit, and she'd be almost old enough to date them!

This wasn't *all* bad.

The other family members moved her aside as they hugged Randy too. Dad thumped him on the back and said it would be the best two years of his life. Mom worried about the list of things they had to buy before he left. Darla told him to be sure to send her a picture of any really cute companions he'd have, which made Marybeth depressed again because who would look at her with Darla around? Still, she'd be going on fifteen when he returned, and she'd have a shape by then. Darla would be nineteen, and maybe already married, so she might not be a problem.

Garth and Grant whapped Randy on the chest and said they'd sure be glad when he was gone because one of them could take his room and they wouldn't have to listen to each other snore anymore. But Marybeth noticed their grins were a little unsteady as they hugged him.

When it was Katie's turn, Randy lifted her right up off her feet and told her sternly not to grow up too fast while he was gone. She giggled and promised she wouldn't.

While they all laughed and chattered together, Marybeth looked at the globe again. Ecuador. Wouldn't there be jungles in Ecuador—dark, tangled masses of trees and vines full of enormous snakes and fat spiders and bats and ghosts of long-dead Spanish explorers?

She shivered. Even girls camp was better than Ecuador.

Was Randy thinking of snakes and bats too, she wondered? His face was flushed and his voice sounded as if he was forcing himself to be happy about his call.

Maybe she could ask him about it later, if she could get him alone for a few minutes. If he confessed that he was terrified to think of those dark

62

jungles, then maybe she could tell him how she felt about going to girls camp, about how she was so afraid of dark places where there were no bright lights. It would be nice to talk to somebody about it. Somebody who would understand.

They finally got around to eating dinner, which Mom had kept warm all this time. There was a lot of laughing and talking around the table and no opportunity to talk alone with Randy. And after they finished eating, Randy went off to tell his buddies about his call.

He wasn't back by the time Marybeth went to bed. As she climbed the stairs, she could hear Mom worrying aloud about how they'd have to get him all outfitted and ready to leave for the Missionary Training Center in just six weeks.

All of this would keep Mom so busy that there was no way she'd be climbing back up to the Limbo Limb in the near future, chair or no chair, so Marybeth's best excuse for not going to camp was for sure wiped out.

She calculated rapidly, determining that Randy would be leaving about two weeks after girls camp was over. There was a still a slim chance that she could say she'd be needed at home during those last weeks before he left. But probably nobody would accept that. And Mom had said she thought his farewell might be held *before* camp.

No. She'd be better off working toward getting Sister Jackson and Brother Turvey to fall in love in a hurry.

She wondered if Sister Jackson would care to play the Guy Game.

The next morning when Marybeth got up, Mom was back up in the tree, sitting again on the lawn chair she'd tied to the Limbo Limb.

Marybeth could scarcely believe her eyes. There must be something really wrong with Mom if she could sit up in the tree when there was so much to do for Randy. It made Marybeth feel very worried about her, but despite her worry there was also a little part of her that was glad. A mother in a tree was still her best excuse not to go to camp.

But it wouldn't hurt to have some back-up excuses, just in case.

This time Marybeth decided to be breezy about the whole situation, so she opened her window and called, "Hi, Mom. How's the air up there this morning?"

Mom looked up from whatever she was doing and smiled. "Fine, honey. It's been a lovely morning."

So how long had she been up there? Had she hoisted herself up there before Dad and Randy left for work? Did they know about it? What if the people in Salt Lake found out about it? Would they cancel Randy's mission call if they knew that his mother spent her mornings sitting high up in a tree?

But Marybeth couldn't worry about that. She had enough problems of her own.

She cleared her throat. "It really is a lovely morning," she said. "So how long are you going to, y'know, be up there?"

Mom didn't answer for quite a while. Then she said, "I can see things so much better from up here." She said it so softly that Marybeth wasn't even sure she heard right. What was it she could see?

Marybeth looked around the familiar neighborhood of houses in orderly rows with neat lawns in front. The San Gabriel mountains, rugged and wrinkled in the early morning sun, were a beautiful backdrop to the whole scene, but Mom wasn't looking at them. She was looking at whatever was in her lap.

She obviously wasn't going to give out any clues.

"I'm going over to Brother Turvey's house," Marybeth called, "as soon as Carlie and the others come. We're going to, y'know, work on our garage sale for camp."

"Good," Mom said without looking up. "I'll have some things I'll contribute to the sale."

With a sigh Marybeth closed the window and got

dressed, putting on a pair of new jeans that needed a little scuffing up before they'd be in shape to wear to school in the fall. Moving Brother Turvey's furniture might wear them down a little.

The other Bee Theres came by just a few minutes before nine o'clock, and they walked together over to Brother Turvey's house. Sister Jackson was already there, standing in the big kitchen with Brother Turvey. They were discussing what furniture would be moved out to make room for the antiques from the attic.

Marybeth was pleased that Sister Jackson was there so early. Maybe it meant she just couldn't stand to be away from Brother Turvey any longer than necessary.

She looked perfect, the way she always did. Even when she was going to scrub and move furniture, she looked perfect. Her pretty white hair was nice and full and curled just right, looking as if she'd never slept on it in her whole life. Marybeth's mom's hair was all flattened out in the morning, but Sister Jackson's was perfect. She was wearing slim brown pants and a white blouse with brown polka dots. She looked fresh and clean and bright, and if Brother Turvey didn't fall in love with her right then and there, he should have his eyes examined.

But it didn't seem as if he needed to have his eyes

examined, the way he was looking at her. And he was agreeing with all the suggestions she was making about the kitchen.

But where was the bread she was supposed to be baking? She'd said she was going to bake bread, and if there was anything that made a kitchen enticing, it was the smell of bread baking.

Marybeth was sure that would send Brother Turvey right over the edge, and that he'd be proposing before the day was over. Then they could get married just in time to disrupt girls camp.

"Would you like me to, y'know, help you mix the bread?" Marybeth asked.

"Oh," Sister Jackson said, "I decided not to do that. I didn't have any yeast, and I didn't want to take time to stop at the store. We'll be too busy to fuss with it anyway. I'll fix something else for lunch."

"My mom always has yeast," Marybeth said quickly. "I'll run home and get some. I really, y'know, love homemade bread." She looked at the other Bee Theres, who picked up her message.

"We all love homemade bread," Carlie said, and the others nodded.

"That was what was going to make all our hard work today worthwhile." Becca looked mournful at the thought of no homemade bread.

They didn't even know how super important this

was to Marybeth, but they were still going right along with her. The Bee Theres really were there when she needed them.

"Well," Sister Jackson said, "I guess I'd better go ahead and make it."

Brother Turvey smiled right along with the Bee Theres.

"Do you have all the other ingredients, Howard?" Sister Jackson asked.

Howard! Things were moving along even better than expected.

"Think so," Brother Turvey said. "Flour, water, salt, sugar, margarine." He opened his refrigerator. "Even got some raspberry jam here that somebody gave me last Christmas. Taste right good with fresh bread."

Sister Jackson turned to Marybeth. "Run get the yeast. We'll get it mixed before we start scrubbing."

Marybeth ran for the kitchen door, but somebody tapped on it before she got it open.

"Come on in," Brother Turvey called. "It's not locked."

Quincy Adkins and Robert Dayton were standing on the little kitchen porch.

"Furniture movers," Quincy said cheerfully. "Ready to work."

There was a third guy with them. Young. About

thirteen or so, Marybeth guessed. Tall. Reddish blond hair like Quincy's.

"Hope you don't mind if we brought my brother along," Quincy said. "He's staying with me for a while. Going to be my assistant when I go to the mountains to cook for girls camp. Name's Sam."

Marybeth just stood there. It was Elena who finally found her voice enough to ask, "You're going to cook at girls camp?"

"Yeah," Quincy said. "I'm grabbing at any jobs that pay money. The regular cook at Camp Cougar quit, so I volunteered since I did that kind of work for a while to earn money for my mission."

Quincy was going to be the cook at camp, and his tall, gorgeous brother Sam was going to be his assistant.

Oh, wow!

Suddenly everything changed, like in a movie when there's a sequence in black and white and then in the next frame it's all in full color.

How could Marybeth not go to girls camp if Sam was going to be there?

But how could she go if she was going to make a fool of herself with her fear about the dark mountains and trees?

What was she going to do now?

CHAPTER
7

Sam was grinning at the Bee Theres, but he looked a little nervous, as if he didn't quite know what to say.

His big brother Quincy must have noticed, because he said, "Sister Jackson and Brother Turvey, this is Sam. Sam, this is Sister Jackson and Brother Turvey."

"Glad to meet you, Sam." Sister Jackson put out her hand, and Sam shook it solemnly.

He and Brother Turvey shook hands too. Then Quincy turned toward the Bee Theres.

Were they supposed to shake hands with Sam too? Marybeth wasn't sure exactly what to do, but she hoped so.

Sam looked as if he was about to break out into a sweat.

"Girls, this is Sam," Quincy said. "Sam, I'd like you to meet Melanie, Julia, Meg, Demi, and Michelle."

The Bee Theres stared blankly at Quincy, who slapped his forehead with the palm of a hand and said, "Oh, sorry. I get them mixed up with movie stars all the time." Grinning broadly, he started over. "Sam, I'd like you to meet Carlie, Elena, Sunshine, Becca, and Maryjane."

"Mary*beth*," Marybeth corrected. She put out her hand the way Sister Jackson had done.

"Mary*beth*," Sam repeated as he reached out to take her hand. His own hand was hard and square, and he had a stick-on tattoo on his arm just above his wrist. It was a snake, coiled up with its head raised.

Sam shook hands with the other Bee Theres, but he didn't say their names. They all stood in a row, blushing just a little so that they looked like a row of bright street lamps.

Marybeth was thrilled. He'd said her name. He'd probably remember it since he'd *said* it.

Now that the introductions were over, Quincy rubbed his hands together. "So where do we start?"

Sister Jackson took charge. "First we need to take some of this furniture out to the garage." She gestured toward the chrome table and chairs and the wrought-iron shelves with the bouquets of dusty silk flowers. "Is that right, Brother Turvey?"

71

"Yes," he said. "You girls can have that stuff for your garage sale."

He wasn't hesitant about it the way he'd been the day before. Marybeth wondered if he'd thought about it the night before and decided that he was going to change his life around. Had he thought about Sister Jackson too, and about really changing his life by marrying her?

"After that we'll all scrub the floors and walls, then move the things from the attic down here," Sister Jackson said. "Oh, and Marybeth, you were going to go back home and get some yeast so we can get that bread baking."

Marybeth hated to leave just then, but the yeast was important so that Sister Jackson could bake the bread that would make Brother Turvey totally fall in love and propose and want to get married during girls camp week so Marybeth wouldn't have to go to the dark mountains.

Suddenly the whole plan seemed flimsy and even silly. Besides, if Sam was going to be at Camp Cougar, she wanted to go, didn't she?

She was about to say she didn't think her mother had any yeast after all when Sister Jackson touched Sam's shoulder and said, "You go with her, Sam, and bring back all the mop buckets Sister Stewart has. Will you do that?"

Sam looked at Marybeth and nodded.

Marybeth could scarcely believe her good luck. Sister Jackson had practically handed Sam to her. She hoped the other Bee Theres didn't mind.

"We'd better go," she said, "so we can, y'know, get back in time to bake the bread."

She avoided looking at Sunshine and Elena and Becca and Carlie as Sam followed her out of the kitchen door. Instead of going cross-lots the way she usually did to get to Brother Turvey's house, she led Sam around the house to the sidewalk. That way would take longer.

Sam didn't say a whole lot for the first block, but maybe that was because Marybeth chattered on about the coming garage sale and how nice Brother Turvey was to let them have all that stuff in the attic. Sam did clear his throat a lot. He seemed kind of shy.

"I like your tattoo," Marybeth said finally, getting away from the subject of the garage sale.

He raised his arm to look at it. "It's fake. I could peel it off if I wanted to."

"Don't peel it," Marybeth said. "I, y'know, like it."

There didn't seem to be anything else to say about the tattoo.

"There's, y'know, a snake at girls camp," she said. "His name's Norman."

Sam nodded. "Quincy told me. Is he real or just, y'know, like a legend or something?"

Was he teasing her with the "y'know" or what? "I think he's real," Marybeth said, taking care not to insert a "y'know" anywhere. "My brothers could tell you. They've been to Camp Cougar when the Scouts were there." She wasn't sure she wanted Sam to meet Garth and Grant yet.

Thinking of her brothers made Marybeth think of home, which made her remember something else. Her mother was still in the tree in the front yard.

What would Sam think when he saw a fully grown mother perched like a bird up there in that tree? Would he decide the whole family must be bonkers and not want to be around Marybeth anymore?

"Let's take a shortcut," she said, leading the way down an alley and across Mrs. Yost's yard.

Sam followed obediently. "Are you really going to, y'know, bake bread today?" he asked.

Marybeth nodded. "Sister Jackson is going to make it."

"I love homemade bread," Sam said. "My grandma used to, y'know, make it, then she died."

"From baking bread?" Marybeth asked.

Sam grinned shyly. "No. She just died. I miss her a lot, and I haven't had homemade bread for, y'know, a long time."

Marybeth decided the "y'know" was just part of his speech, the way it was with her. It gave them something in common.

She vowed that she was going to learn to make bread. Maybe she could be the bread baker at girls camp and spend the time in the kitchen with Quincy and Sam rather than going off in the dark woods to complete the badge requirements and all that stuff they'd been learning about.

Maybe she could even get over being scared of the dark so that she'd enjoy going to girls camp, especially if Sam was there. Maybe sometime she'd throw away the night light she'd smuggled into her room. Or at least maybe she'd not plug it in the way she did every night when she didn't think anybody would be coming into her room anymore.

But she wouldn't do it that night.

Garth and Grant were both in the kitchen when Marybeth and Sam got to her house. They had their heads in the refrigerator, searching for something to eat even though they must have just had breakfast.

The twins glanced briefly at Sam, throwing a muffled "Hi" at him before returning their gaze to the refrigerator.

"Hi," Sam said to their backs. He cleared his throat. "Marybeth said you guys know all about the, y'know, snake at Camp Cougar."

"Yip," Garth said.

Sam looked puzzled.

Marybeth wanted to tell Garth that it was okay to yip at her "y'knows," but that he should stifle it when it came to Sam.

"We know all about that snake," Grant said, slowly turning around to face Sam. "Don't we?" He poked Garth.

"We do-hoo," Garth said.

Marybeth glared at him, trying to tell him to cut out the echo stuff, too. Her family was so embarrassing.

"Sit down," Grant said, waving a hand at the kitchen chairs. "What did you say your name is?"

"Sam," Sam said.

"Sam." Garth repeated the name. "Well, Sam, you've come to the right place to learn about Norman, the eighty-foot snake who swallows small children whole."

"Bigger people he has to chew on for a while," Grant added.

Marybeth didn't want to hear it. She got a package of yeast from the refrigerator, put it in her pocket, and hurried out to the utility room, where she searched until she found three plastic pails that would serve as mop buckets. Pulling out a stack of old rags Mom kept in a drawer, she dropped them into one pail and hurried back to the kitchen.

Garth and Grant were just warming up on their snake stories. Grant was talking. "Did you hear about the time Norman singlehandedly . . . "

"So to speak," Garth interrupted. "Snakes don't have hands, single or otherwise."

"I know that," Grant said.

"Single *snakedly*," Garth suggested.

"How Norman single *snakedly* wiped out a whole Boy Scout troop?" Grant finished.

Garth nodded. "We were there."

When Sam saw Marybeth come back with the pails, he stood up. "Guess we'd better, y'know, get back to Brother Turvey's."

"Yip," Garth said.

Sam looked a little wild-eyed. Marybeth figured she'd better get him out of there.

"Come on, Sam." She handed him a couple of pails and headed toward the front door. She wasn't sure what Garth and Grant would do if she led Sam to the back door, which meant passing close to where they sat. She should never have brought him inside without checking to see if Garth and Grant were there.

She and Sam were all the way out of the front

door before she remembered that her mom was still up on the Limbo Limb.

Sam spotted her before Marybeth could scuttle him past the tree.

"Who's that?" he whispered.

Marybeth's face burned. "My mom." She didn't even attempt an explanation.

They were silent as they hurried along the street, heading back to Brother Turvey's house.

But Marybeth couldn't help but notice that Sam shifted both buckets to the same hand so that he could use the other to peel the snake tattoo from his arm and drop it in the gutter.

CHAPTER
8

The Bee Theres already had part of the kitchen floor and walls scrubbed when Marybeth and Sam got back to Brother Turvey's.

"We left that part for you, Marybeth," Becca said, pointing to the wall between the windows where the hoosier was going to stand. She sounded cranky.

Maybe she was angry that Marybeth and Sam had been gone for quite a while. Or maybe she hadn't had any breakfast or something.

Marybeth gave the yeast to Sister Jackson, then filled one of the buckets with suds and got to work.

The bread was baking by the time the kitchen was clean to Sister Jackson's specifications. The aroma gave the whole house a cozy, warm feeling. Marybeth saw Sam sniff the air several times, but he didn't say anything.

What had happened to him? He'd seemed so friendly on the way over to her house. It was probably those rotten twins, Garth and Grant, and what they'd been saying that had changed him. That and seeing Mom sitting up in the tree. He probably thought her whole family was nutsy.

The other Bee Theres worked silently too, not speaking to Marybeth. What was the matter with them?

"All right," Sister Jackson said when they had wrung out their scrubbing rags and set the buckets aside. "Now let's bring down the furniture." She turned to look at Marybeth and the other Bee Theres. "You girls can carry down the small stuff we're going to use in here. Then you can sort through the things you want for your garage sale."

Brother Turvey had rigged up a better light for the attic, so it wasn't so frightening to be there now. It didn't take long to bring down the small stuff—an old brass lamp, a small pine knickknack shelf, the brown pot Brother Turvey said his mother had used for flowers, an old picture of a lone wolf standing on a snowy hillside overlooking a small town. Brother Turvey said his mother had liked that picture.

Sister Jackson asked Brother Turvey where things had been in his mother's kitchen. Then she had all of the furniture put in approximately the same place in this one. A whole different kitchen began to appear right before everybody's eyes.

Now that the things Brother Turvey wanted were gone from the attic, the Bee Theres were free to look through the remaining stuff for saleable items. There were clothes and still-good leather purses and books and dishes and costume jewelry and lots of other items that would be great for the garage sale. Sunshine and Becca and Elena and Carlie commented on the things they found, but Marybeth couldn't help but notice they didn't include her.

She was digging in an old trunk. "Hey, look at this," she said, holding up a long coat with a big fur collar. "Maybe we should keep this for a costume for the Halloween spook alley."

The other Bee Theres glanced at it.

Sunshine shrugged. "If you want it," she said.

The others didn't seem interested. They didn't say anything.

It was as if Marybeth had been cut away from them. Why? What had she done?

She was trying to decide whether or not to come right out and ask, when Sister Jackson called up to them.

"Lunch," Sister Jackson said. "Come get washed up."

Silently they all went down to eat.

Three fat loaves of bread sat on the counter in a kitchen that had been totally transformed. The old wood of the hoosier and the buffet and the round table glowed softly in the noonday light as if it had all just been rubbed with lemon oil, which it probably had.

Sister Jackson had found a soft orange-and-white-checked tablecloth somewhere, and she had set the big oak table with Sister Turvey's brown earthenware dishes. She'd picked some yellow daisies from Brother Turvey's yard and had put them in the center in the brown pot.

Brother Turvey was circling around saying, "Oh, my. Oh, my!"

His eyes followed Sister Jackson as she cut thick slices of bread and took a huge garden salad and the jar of raspberry jam from the refrigerator. Marybeth figured it was a sure thing that he was already in love with Sister Jackson. He seemed very ready to start on the new life he had talked about.

That was nice, but it wasn't important to Marybeth any more. *Her* life was falling apart. Now that she had decided to somehow overcome her fear of dark places and go to girls camp where Sam would be, he wasn't even talking to her. Wouldn't even look at her. And the other Bee Theres had all but thrown her out of the club.

"Marybeth, will you stop daydreaming and sit down?" Becca said sharply.

Marybeth came back to reality and saw that Sister Jackson was looking at her and pointing out where she should sit. She had to get to a chair back against the wall before the other Bee Theres could sit down.

Quickly she slipped past chairs to get to the place assigned to her. She was just a little ticked off at Becca for calling attention to the fact that she'd been spacing out. Sam was going to know she was as goofed up as the rest of her family.

Sister Jackson had put a leaf in the table so there was plenty of room for everybody. Sam sat across from Marybeth, with Quincy and Robert on either side of him. Sister Jackson and Brother Turvey sat side by side next to Quincy, and the Bee Theres filled in the rest of the spaces.

They were like a big happy family sitting down for a meal. Except no one seemed especially happy, except for Brother Turvey and Sister Jackson. And Quincy and Robert, who were kidding about the hernias the heavy furniture had caused.

"Can't you shift over a little," Carlie said to Marybeth, "so your elbow won't be right in my plate?"

Sunshine snatched a napkin practically right out of Marybeth's hand when she reached for the wrong one.

Sam, across the table, was looking at his plate or at the ceiling or anywhere but at her.

Brother Turvey harrumphed a couple of times and said, "In my house we always hold hands around the table while we say the blessing on the food."

He reached for Sister Jackson's hand on his one side and for Quincy's on the other.

It seemed to Marybeth that Sunshine and Becca hesitated a little before they took hold of the hands she held out.

Then the circle was complete and Brother Turvey began saying the blessing. He gave thanks for the beautiful day and for the General Authorities in Salt Lake and for the missionaries out preaching to the world. He gave instructions that a special blessing be visited upon the President of the United States and other government leaders who needed guidance in these perilous times. He went on to give thanks for the stake president and the bishop and finally narrowed it down to the special friends who sat around his table. About the time Becca and Sunshine began to twitch, Marybeth heard him finish up with gratitude for the hands that had prepared the meal and for the food itself, and after everybody had said amen, they began to eat.

"Best bread I ever ate," Quincy pronounced after biting into a slice generously slathered with butter.

Marybeth was surprised the bread was still hot, after the sermon-length blessing on the food. But it was good, especially with a thin layer of raspberry jam on top of the butter.

"Is this as good as your grandma used to make?" she asked Sam across the table in an attempt to get him back to talking.

"Yes," he said without looking at her.

"How about giving bread-baking lessons, Sister Jackson?" Quincy said.

"I'd be happy to," Sister Jackson said with a pleased smile.

Marybeth remembered her earlier thoughts that maybe she could bake bread at girls camp.

"I'd like to learn how to do it," she said. "Then I could help in the kitchen at Camp Cougar."

The other Bee Theres glared at her, and she knew they knew why she wanted to be in the kitchen. They seemed mad about the fact that she'd got to know Sam before they did. They were always complaining about how she was always the first one to talk to any guys they met and how she was such a flirt.

But that was only partly true. She talked to guys because she had four older brothers. Guys didn't seem as threatening to her as they did to the others who weren't around them all the time.

Or could it be that she really *was* a flirt?

Maybe they could talk about it when they got together for dinner at McDonald's that evening.

Sister Jackson was speaking. "I'm afraid you wouldn't be allowed to work in the kitchen at camp, Marybeth. You'll have your badges to earn, and besides, mingling with the young men who are there is strictly forbidden. As far as you're concerned, you're to regard them as trees and not to be spoken to."

Trees! She should regard Sam as a tree?

Well, then there wasn't any purpose at all in overcoming her fear of dark places, because she for sure wasn't going to camp.

When Marybeth got home after eating a big dish of Sister Jackson's homemade ice cream, her mother was no longer up on the Limbo Limb. She was sitting at the kitchen table, writing something on a pad of yellow paper.

She looked up when Marybeth came through the door.

"Hi, honey," she said. "Everything go all right at Brother Turvey's?"

Marybeth nodded. "He gave us a lot of stuff for our garage sale."

"Good. Remind me to root out some things for

you when I have time." She tapped the yellow paper with her pencil. "I'm making a list of what has to be done before Randy goes on his mission. I called the bishop, and, as I suspected, Randy's farewell sacrament meeting will be on the Sunday before you go to girls camp because other things are already scheduled on the other Sundays."

Whatever. It didn't matter. "Fine, Mom," Marybeth said. "Where are Garth and Grant?"

Mom motioned with her head toward the backyard. "Supposed to be mowing grass and trimming shrubs, but I don't hear any motors. Want to go tell them to get with it?"

Marybeth knew they wouldn't pay any attention to orders delivered by her, but she said, "Sure, Mom," and went looking for them.

They were lounging in the shade of the pomegranate tree, licking at ice cream cones they'd probably got from the ice cream truck that came by every day.

"Hi," Marybeth said. She wanted to keep it friendly until she could learn what she wanted.

"Hey, Twerp." Grant waved his ice cream. "Where'd your clone go?"

"Clone?" She didn't know what he meant.

"Yeah," Grant said. "The, y'know, guy who was,

y'know, with you when you, y'know, came for the, y'know, buckets."

"Yip, yip, yip, yip," Garth said.

It took all of Marybeth's willpower not to stomp away. The twins were totally totaled out. "I don't know." She shrugged as if it didn't matter to her where he was. "I guess he's gone to Quincy Adkin's place. He's visiting Quincy."

"Yeah?" Grant seemed mildly interested. "Quincy's all right. He's our new quorum adviser."

"Sam's his brother." Marybeth was careful not to say any y'knows. "What was all that stuff you were telling him while I was looking for buckets?"

Garth grinned. "You mean about Norman?"

"We were just warning him about Norman and all the other snakes there at Camp Cougar," Grant said. "Told him a sleeping bag without a snake is like a cone without ice cream." He held up his cone.

"Like ketchup without fries," Garth added. "Like frosting without cake. An essential ingredient is missing if you don't have a snake in your sleeping bag at good old Camp Cougar."

Grant sat up to peer at Marybeth. "Why'd you want to know? Did good old Sam freak out about Norman?"

"Of course not." But Marybeth wasn't so sure. Was that why Sam had been so quiet? Or was it just because the dumb twins had gotten to him with their yipping whenever he said "y'know"?

Or had it been because he saw Marybeth's mother up in the tree?

"Aren't you guys supposed to be working?" Marybeth asked, not minding that her irritation with them showed through as she turned to stomp back to the house.

The other Bee Theres were already sitting around a table when Marybeth got to McDonald's for dinner, as they'd agreed to do yesterday. They were all kind of leaning in toward each other as if they were saying things they didn't want anybody else to hear.

When they looked up and saw her, their faces were like closed doors. As if they had just decided they were not going to let her into their little circle.

Marybeth felt hot, then cold. Cold as ice, as if she'd been thrust into outer darkness. Darkness much worse than that back at the old farm in Utah.

CHAPTER
9

There were only four chairs around the table. It was as if the other Bee Theres had already voted Marybeth out of the group and left room only for the four of them.

Well, she wasn't going to let it be that easy.

She grabbed an empty chair from a nearby table. "Mind if I join you?" she asked pleasantly, pushing it between Sunshine and Carlie.

Becca shrugged. "If you want to."

Marybeth sat down.

"We already have our food." Elena held up her Big Mac. "We weren't exactly sure you were coming." She sounded a little apologetic.

"Why *wouldn't* I come?" Marybeth asked.

"Maybe you had other interests?" Becca seemed

uncomfortable as Marybeth stared at her. "Or something. You know. Other things to do."

Sunshine was braver than Becca. "Like going off with Sam."

She wilted as Marybeth turned to look at her.

"Or something," she finished.

Marybeth was ticked off. Why were they treating her like this? "Why would I go off with Sam or anybody else when we had a Bee Theres meeting scheduled?"

The others looked at their food.

"Why don't you just tell me what's really wrong?" Marybeth said softly.

Elena laid down her Big Mac. "Marybeth, it's just that, I mean, it's like whenever there's a boy around you just jump right in and grab him."

"Every time we see a guy, you start talking to him before we even get to say a word," Sunshine complained.

Carlie nodded. "Every time."

"Yeah," Becca said. "You just go ahead and hog all the guys."

Now it was if somebody had opened a lid and all the bad things were escaping.

"You're boy crazy," Sunshine said. "Guy ga-ga. Man-struck."

"The rest of us don't have a chance," Carlie said.

"You just carry them off." Elena gave Marybeth a belligerent look as she said it.

It was just as Marybeth had suspected. They were jealous.

"Hey," she said, "why don't *you* talk to a guy when one comes around? Who's stopping you?"

Nobody said anything.

"Well," Marybeth said, "why?"

Carlie shifted uncomfortably. "I don't know what to say to a guy when I meet him."

"I don't either," admitted Sunshine.

"I'm too shy," Elena said.

Becca glared at Marybeth. "By the time I open my mouth, you're already talking to him."

Marybeth bent her head for a moment, thinking. Why wasn't *she* afraid to talk to boys? Why could *she* always think of something to say? Well, it was because of what she'd been thinking about earlier.

"Listen," she said. "I've got four older brothers. They've been around my whole life. I don't have any problem talking to them. So I guess I figure other guys are pretty much like my brothers, and I just talk to them the same way I'd talk to Brad and Randy and Garth and Grant."

The other Bee Theres were silent as they thought about that.

"If you had older brothers, you'd be the same way," Marybeth added.

"I have an older brother," Becca said. "I guess I never really thought of him as being a *guy.*"

"Other girls think he's a guy," Marybeth said, "even though to you he's only a brother."

That seemed to make sense to the other Bee Theres. They sat back and began eating again.

"You'd better get your food," Elena said. "We need to talk about our bridesmaid dresses for Pamela's wedding. That's what we're here for."

Suddenly the whole mood changed.

"That's going to be so fun," Sunshine said.

They all smiled, and Marybeth felt that their problem with her was already forgotten.

But she wasn't going to forget it. At least she wouldn't forget how she'd felt when she'd been an outcast. She didn't want to feel that way again.

Which meant that there was no way she could *not* go to camp with the others. If she used one of her many excuses to stay home, then they would be doing something she would not be a part of. They would come home talking about all their camp experiences, and she would be an outsider because she hadn't been there. Things would never be quite the same again if she didn't go.

On the other hand, if she went and they found

out how she was such a baby about the dark, how she was terrified when all the lights went out, then she'd be an outcast again anyway.

Which was worse?

"After we decide about the dresses, let's talk about camp," she said as she stood up to go get her food. Maybe then she'd find the answer to her dilemma.

It took a long time to decide about the bridesmaids' dresses for Pamela's wedding. They all finished their Big Macs and fries and shakes and still hadn't settled anything.

Each girl wanted a different color. That was the problem.

Becca, with her red hair, wanted green dresses. Carlie thought a vivid blue would go best with her black hair. Elena said red was best with her coloring of black hair and olive skin. Purple was Marybeth's favorite color, and it went well with her brown hair. Sunshine, a blond, wanted pink.

"Pink would kill me," Becca said.

Carlie shuddered at the thought of green.

"I can't wear blue," Elena said.

Sunshine pointed down her throat and made a gagging sound at the thought of purple.

"Red makes me feel like a fire hydrant," Marybeth said.

"We can't all wear different colors," Becca said. "Unless Pamela wants a rainbow wedding."

Carlie groaned. "We're just going to have to figure out what looks good on all of us."

"Let's think about what Pamela would like," Marybeth said. "What are her best colors?"

"Orange," Elena said. "She wears a lot of orange."

Becca shook her head. "I'd die in orange."

"That's not a good wedding color anyway," Sunshine said. "Can you imagine a wedding cake decorated in bright orange?"

"Neon orange, with the top lit up." Elena giggled as she said it.

"Let's think about Pamela," Carlie said. "What does she remind you of?"

Becca closed her eyes. "Firelight."

"A summer sunset when the sky is all orangey," Elena offered.

"A peach," Marybeth said.

"Peach!" Sunshine hit the table with her hand. "What about a nice, warm peach color for our dresses?"

They looked at one another.

"We all look good in peach," Carlie said.

"Good for you, Marybeth," Elena said.

It was decided. They would suggest peach-colored dresses to Pamela. They would all be dressed alike. The Bee Theres, all for one and one for all.

Marybeth didn't know when she'd ever felt so happy. Once more she was part of them. She didn't ever want to be an outcast again. Which meant she was going to have to go to camp with the others. Somehow she was going to have to find a way to overcome her fear of the dark.

"Maybe," Becca said, "we can wear the same dresses for Sister Jackson's wedding."

They all giggled.

"Do you really think she'll marry Brother Turvey?" Sunshine asked.

Becca raised her eyebrows. "Are you kidding? I don't think he's going to let her even leave that new-old kitchen she's fixed up for him."

"Speaking of Brother Turvey," Marybeth said, "even with all the stuff he gave us, we don't have enough for our garage sale. We'd better plan how we're going to get more."

They sat at the table for another hour deciding how they were going to accumulate more garage-sale items. They would put an item in the ward bulletin on Sunday. They would go door-to- door through their neighborhoods, asking if anyone had anything to contribute.

They sat there so long that one of the cute guys from behind the counter walked past and asked if they were putting down roots.

Marybeth was about to say, "Yes, and we're about to branch out to another table," but she bit her tongue and held it back. She waited for one of the others to say something to him, but they all just giggled and ducked their heads.

Well, this time she'd given them the chance. They couldn't say she'd hogged that guy too.

The weeks began to speed by as the Bee Theres collected things for their garage sale. Everybody in the ward seemed to have something to contribute, and the pile in Brother Turvey's garage grew.

Sister Jackson spent a lot of time with them, sorting through the stuff and putting on price stickers. Brother Turvey, too, seemed to find lots to do in the garage. The Bee Theres figured he just wanted to be near Sister Jackson.

One day when they were all walking to Albertson's for ice cream cones, they saw the two of them, all dressed up, go down the street in Brother Turvey's car.

"They're going on a date," Becca whispered, and

the Bee Theres wondered aloud when the wedding would be.

"At least we know it's not the same week as camp," Marybeth said, since Sister Jackson had told them she would be going to camp with them.

Sunshine gave her a puzzled look. "What makes you think she'd ever set her wedding for camp week even if she wasn't going with us?"

Marybeth had forgotten that the others didn't know she'd once hoped Sister Jackson and Brother Turvey would get married that week so none of them could go to camp.

"Just kidding," Marybeth said.

Marybeth didn't see much of Sam during the passing weeks. He came to church with Quincy every Sunday, but he hung out with the other deacons. He didn't talk to her, but he didn't talk to the other Bee Theres either.

At home, her mom still climbed up to the Limbo Limb in the front yard tree every day for at least a couple of hours. It got so that she was just part of the scenery there in the neighborhood, and people would stop to talk to her if they were passing by. They'd stand underneath the tree with their heads tipped back and their mouths open.

Marybeth still worried about her and wondered what she did up there, but now she didn't need her as an excuse not to go to camp. She was going to go.

Randy got his hair cut and bought some dark missionary suits and white shirts. One day he asked Marybeth to go shopping with him to help him pick out some ties.

"You've got a good eye for a great tie," he said.

She giggled. "You're a poet and don't know it," she retorted.

She was glad to go with him because there were just the two of them, and as they drove to the mall she finally had a chance to ask him if he was unhappy about going to Ecuador rather than Germany.

He gave her a surprised look. "Don't you remember what we sang before I opened my mission papers, Twerp?" He cleared his throat and, faking a high tenor, warbled, "I'll go where you want me to go, dear Lord, over mountain or plain or sea."

"But you looked, y'know, disappointed or something when you read that you were going to Ecuador."

"You're very observant, Twerp. Nobody else noticed. But it wasn't disappointment. I was scared. Still am. I don't know if I can measure up to this. You know, going off to a country I've hardly even heard of and learning a language I know two words of and living with guys I've never met and trying to tell people something they might not want to hear."

Marybeth couldn't believe what she was hearing. Randy, her big, handsome, athletic, confident brother, scared of going on his mission.

"Scared?" she squeaked.

"Scared," he said.

She almost blurted out that she was scared too. Scared of the dark and what might be there. What she couldn't see. Things that might come out of the darkness, like the ghost that had appeared out of the murky blackness at the old historical farm in Utah.

But they were at the mall then, and Randy was parking the car. Her confession would have to wait, if she decided to tell him what she'd not told anybody else.

As they walked into the Broadway, past the purse counter and the junior department where there were some to-die-for jeans on display, she thought about how she'd tell him on the way home. It would be such a relief to talk to somebody about it. Especially Randy, who was scared about something too.

She was so deep in her thoughts that she hardly saw the two guys standing there in the men's department, looking at shirts. One was Quincy, and the other was Sam.

Or at least she thought it was Sam. He wasn't

there long because he suddenly disappeared behind a rack of suits.

She was sure he'd seen her. But he'd deliberately slid right out of her sight.

She was an outcast again, rejected by Sam, who didn't even want to look at her. She was so depressed on the way home that she didn't tell Randy about being afraid of the dark anyway.

CHAPTER
10

For a change, nobody in Marybeth's family had anything to complain about on Gripe Night that evening. Dad could hardly believe it, and said maybe all his efforts to head his family in the right direction were paying off.

Nobody mentioned that Mom still spent her days up in the tree, and Marybeth wondered if Dad even knew about it. She really didn't seem any different when she was down out of the tree, so she must be all right.

When Marybeth went to bed, a familiar dream came back. She was at the old farm again, and it was a dark night, hot and smothering, with no light anywhere except from the stars. She was there in the old farmhouse, listening to the creaks and groans of the ancient wooden walls. The ghost was there, hanging white and silent and sad in the darkness.

No, it was Sam who was there, and they weren't in the farmhouse at all. They were in the barn, and he was grinning at her over the back of a cow. He glided into a horse stall, where he picked up a snake and wrapped it around his arm. It slithered up around his neck and down into his shirt. Then he was running, peeking at her from among the tall stalks of corn in the garden the way he'd peered at her through the racks of men's suits at the Broadway.

And Mom was there in front of the old house, roosting atop a tall poplar, cawing like an enormous crow, and sewing camp name tags in Randy's new white missionary shirts.

Marybeth woke up hot and sweaty, her heart drumming hollowly in her chest.

Someone had turned out her night light!

Choking with fright, she sat up, and the edge of the sheet that had been covering her eyes slipped away.

The light was on after all. She could see the familiar outlines of her furniture and the clothes she'd left on a chair. She reached out and turned on her bedside lamp, taking deep breaths to slow down her thumping heart.

What if the dream came while she was at camp?

What if she woke up and it was totally dark and she screamed and sobbed and showed all the girls in the whole entire stake what a big blubbery baby she was?

If that happened, she'd have to move away. She'd have to go live with relatives in Wyoming or somewhere else far away and never come back where they'd point fingers and taunt her about being a wimpy fraidy-cat.

She couldn't go to camp!

But how could she get out of it? Mom seemed to be okay when she was out of the tree, so that wasn't such a good excuse. The romance between Sister Jackson and Brother Turvey didn't seem to be going fast enough to interfere with camp.

She'd have to go.

Unless, of course, the Bee Theres didn't make enough money from their garage sale to pay for everybody in the class to go. Then she could still say she'd stay home, and they'd all think she was unselfish and noble, and she'd probably be asked to give a speech in the next stake conference about giving up something for the benefit of somebody else. She might even get her picture in the stake newspaper.

Maybe it would rain on the day of the garage sale. Maybe nobody would see the signs they'd put up and nobody would come to buy anything.

She could still hope for that. The garage sale was still a week away. She could pray every night for it to be a miserable failure.

She decided to go back to sleep, but not before she got up and looked under the bed, just to make sure nothing was lurking there. Before she drifted off, she thought about Sam again, and the way he'd hid from her. Why had he disappeared like that when he saw her? She could have understood it if he'd been buying underwear or something embarrassing, but he and Quincy had been merely looking at T-shirts.

She'd liked him so much the first day they'd met, when he'd walked with her over to her house. He'd seemed to like her too, at first. What had gone wrong?

Sighing, she turned over and went to sleep.

The next day was Saturday, and it was a family rule on most Saturdays that they all eat breakfast together and help clean up the house for Sunday before going off to do anything else.

Mom didn't climb up in the tree on weekends. She went there only Monday through Friday, as if she had a weekday job up there amid the leaves and branches and twigs.

She made waffles this Saturday, with fresh peaches on top. As they all sat down to eat, Randy said, "The bishop talked to me about my farewell. He asked if I thought all of you would be willing to speak at it next week."

Dad nodded and said, "I think it would be an honor for the whole family to be on the program," but there were yelps of horror from Garth and Grant.

"No way," Garth said, shaking his head so hard you could almost hear his brain rattle. "You can't make me stand up there in front of the whole congregation and make a fool of myself."

"Ditto-ho," Grant said. "No way."

They had all been asked to speak at their oldest brother Brad's farewell almost four years ago, and Garth and Grant, only ten then, hadn't been able to say a word when they stood behind the pulpit. In fact, Garth had burst into tears, bawling away until Brad got up and said Garth was just overcome by the thoughts of Brad's leaving. It wasn't the truth, because he was letting the twins use his telescope while he was on his mission, and they'd counted the days until he'd be gone.

When their oldest sister, Barbara, went on her mission, she had had a very short farewell, just Mom and Dad and her and the bishop speaking. Marybeth suspected that she just didn't want to chance a replay of that rainy scene by the twins.

But with Randy's farewell, it wasn't going to be that easy on them.

"Okay," Randy said, "but if you don't speak, I'll give my room to Mom while I'm gone."

"To Mom! What would *she* do with it?" Grant asked.

"I'd love to have it," Mom said quickly.

Garth and Grant both looked at her as if they'd never seen her before.

Marybeth looked at her too. Did she sit up in the tree because she didn't have anywhere else to do whatever it was she did up there?

No. She had lots of space in the big room she shared with Dad. And their house was big.

"Why do you want Randy's room?" Garth said.

"Pass the peaches," Mom said. "Would anybody like more waffles?"

Why *did* she want Randy's room?

"I'll, y'know, speak at your farewell, Randy," Marybeth said.

She waited for Garth to yip about the "y'know." She'd been really watching her speech lately, so there hadn't been that many. He should have pounced on it.

But Garth didn't say anything. He and Grant were whispering together and didn't even seem to notice.

"I knew I could count on you, Twerp," Randy said. "How about you, Katie?"

Katie's eight-year-old cheeks were full of waffles, pouched out like a chipmunk's.

"Sure," she said casually, as if she gave speeches in church every day of the week.

Darla put up her hand. "Me, too. I'll tell everybody about you know what."

Randy gave her a startled look. "You wouldn't!"

Darla nodded. "I would."

Marybeth waited to hear about "you know what." But Randy, after grinning at Darla for a moment, said, "That's your choice, but be prepared for the consequences." He turned back to the twins. "What about it, guys? No speech, no room."

"We'll have to think about it," Garth said.

"Okay," Randy said, "but I have to let the bishop know what you decide. He's anxious to get everything set up for the meeting."

Marybeth was surprised at the twins' reaction. Garth and Grant had been talking for months about each having a room to himself. They must be really seriously terrified if they'd even consider giving it up.

It was something to think about, the twins being afraid of something like that.

Sunday went by fast. There weren't many Sundays left before Randy would be leaving for the Missionary Training Center in Provo, where he'd spend several weeks learning Spanish before he went to Ecuador. Monday and Tuesday rushed by too, and the rest of the week went just as fast.

Saturday, the day of the garage sale, dawned bright and clear, much to Marybeth's disappointment. Sister Jackson and the Bee Theres had worked hard all day Friday, getting everything sorted out on tables in Brother Turvey's garage. They'd tacked signs to trees on street corners for several blocks around.

The sale was supposed to start at eight o'clock, but the Bee Theres got to Brother Turvey's house early. Sister Jackson's car was already out in front with a big sign on top saying, "Garage sale! Here! Today!"

"She's sure over here a lot," Sunshine whispered.

"Well, they're in love," declared Carlie.

The garage door was still closed, keeping all the sale things safe, but the front door to the house was open. The Bee Theres went inside, walking silently across the thick carpeting of the living room. They could smell the aroma of baking bread. It made Marybeth's stomach growl even though she'd had breakfast. The kitchen door was open and they could see Sister Jackson standing at the counter cutting something.

"Come over here, Howard," she said.

He came to her, smiling and reaching out his arms.

"He's going to kiss her," Becca whispered.

The Bee Theres held their breath, their eyes wide.

But Brother Turvey didn't kiss her after all. Instead, he took a large basket she handed to him and headed for the garage.

"Put it on the table with the checked spread," Sister Jackson said. "Then everybody who comes can have a piece of bread while they shop."

The Bee Theres began breathing again. They looked at one another with disappointment. Marybeth knew they'd all wanted to witness a romantic scene between Brother Turvey and Sister Jackson. But it hadn't happened.

"Oh, hello, girls," Sister Jackson said, glancing up and seeing her class standing there. "Come on in. I've been baking bread this morning. Nothing peps up a house or a garage sale like the smell of something good cooking."

Marybeth's heart sank. It certainly didn't seem as if their sale was going to be a failure. The smell—and taste—of that bread was going to make everybody buy like crazy.

And that's what happened. People started arriving even before eight o'clock, and one woman, after eating three pieces of warm bread and raspberry jam, paid one hundred dollars for an old chest that had been in Brother Turvey's attic.

When they'd brought it downstairs, Marybeth had wondered who would want a beat-up old piece of furniture like that, all scarred and scratched and painted white. But the woman had carefully examined the inside of the drawers and the back of the chest and had said it was solid oak there underneath the paint. She wrote out the check and happily carried it away.

So the Bee Theres had one-fifth of the money they needed even before the sale officially opened.

That's the way it went all day. The Bee Theres were kept busy modeling straw hats and holding up dresses so customers could view them, and playing old records and tapes on a sound system Brother Turvey had set up for demonstrations.

People liked shopping in the little garage that had been converted into a store. Sister Jackson had encouraged the Bee Theres to display things attractively on shelves and tables. The old jewelry they'd gathered from various ward members looked terrific spread around on a dark green tablecloth. There was a comfortable chair, also for sale, alongside the bookshelf so a person could sit down to read for a while before buying. A card table was set up as if it was all ready for lunch, and somebody bought the donated dishes on it right away.

Sister Jackson kept baking fresh bread all day long, and Brother Turvey kept the basket on the checked tablecloth filled at all times.

People paid for and carried away old chairs, bed frames, knickknacks, tools, picture frames, toys. Somebody even tried to buy the basket the bread was in.

By the time it was over, the Bee Theres counted $517.17 from the shoe box where they'd put the money as it came in.

"We made enough for everybody," Marybeth said. "We can all go to camp."

Sister Jackson looked surprised. "There was never any question about that. If we hadn't made enough, the ward would have filled in the gap. I thought you knew that."

Marybeth groaned silently. She might as well have faced up weeks ago to the fact that nothing was going to save her from going to camp. Now there was just Randy's farewell, and then she'd be shipped off to those dark mountains.

CHAPTER
11

Marybeth went to bed earlier than usual that night. It was a good time to try sleeping without her night light since she was tired from the garage sale and would probably not wake up while it was dark. If she practiced sleeping without the light all week, then she might be able to survive the dark nights at girls camp.

Everybody except Katie was still up. Randy and Darla had gone to a dance over in Glendora, the last one Randy would be attending until he came home from his mission. Mom was at the kitchen table preparing her family living lesson for Relief Society. Dad was asleep in his reclining chair in front of the TV, which was playing an old western movie with an actor named John Wayne. The twins were in Randy's room, probably trying to decide if having rooms of their own was worth the terror of speaking at his farewell next Sunday.

Marybeth yawned as she told everybody good-night. She really was tired. The Bee Theres had helped Sister Jackson put Brother Turvey's garage back in order after the sale. They'd put the leftover things in boxes for whoever decided next to have a garage sale, washed the dishes and pans Sister Jackson had used for the bread baking, and straightened up the cozy kitchen.

It had been a long day, and when Marybeth closed her eyes in her dark room, she knew she'd go right to sleep even without her night light.

But she didn't. She kept hearing strange noises. The air-conditioning system came on with a soft hiss. A dog barked outside. Did their house always creak as it cooled off from the hot day? Somebody was talking softly. Or was it just the TV muttering downstairs? Or was it . . . was it . . .

Marybeth didn't dare open her eyes. Ruby's ghost might be standing there in the room, white and faintly luminous the way it had been back at the old historical farm.

Or worse, the ghost of Brother Turvey's wife might appear, demanding to know why the Bee Theres had sold so many of her things to strangers.

Marybeth's heart pounded. Wimp, she told herself. Wimpy baby, afraid of the dark.

Sliding out of bed, she plugged in the night light, and when she lay down again she went to sleep immediately.

The next day in church the bishop announced that Randy's farewell would be the following Sunday. Marybeth saw Garth and Grant, who were on the front bench waiting to pass the sacrament, slide down in their seats. They must have decided they'd speak at the farewell, and they were already overcome with terror.

But their talks would be short and then their terror would be over. Girls camp was five whole days. Five whole nights!

Marybeth didn't realize she'd groaned aloud until several people turned to look at her.

Mom leaned across Katie to say, "Are you all right?"

Marybeth nodded, coughing a couple of times as if that explained the groan.

Sister Jackson and Brother Turvey were sitting together on one of the center pews. Marybeth tried to see if they were holding hands or anything, but she couldn't tell. Had they decided yet that they were going to get married? Would Sister Jackson be making an announcement in their Beehive class that day?

115

She didn't. She started the class as usual, with Marybeth, who was class president, conducting the opening exercises.

Marybeth chose Elena to say the prayer since she always said such good ones, and Marybeth needed all the help she could get if she was really going to go through with the camp thing. Next she asked Carlie to repeat the Young Women theme, since she was the one who had memorized it the best.

Carlie stood up and without even faltering said, *"We are daughters of our Heavenly Father who loves us, and we love him. We will 'stand as witnesses of God at all times and in all things, and in all places . . . ' as we strive to live the Young Women Values, which are: Faith, Divine Nature, Individual Worth, Knowledge, Choice and Accountability, Good Works and Integrity."*

For the first time the "choice" part leaped out at Marybeth. Did she have a choice about girls camp?

No.

Yes.

She could choose not to go, even now.

But what about the "accountability" part? Wasn't that like when Darla had said she was going to tell something about Randy in her sacrament meeting talk and he'd said, "That's your choice, but be prepared for the consequences"?

Marybeth had already thought about the consequences of not going to camp. She'd be an outcast if she didn't go.

She'd be an outcast if she *did* go.

When the preliminaries were finished and Sister Jackson took over the class, she let them talk about camp for a while.

Elena was worried about something. "What if we don't all get in the same cabin?" she asked. "What if we're all in different cabins?"

Marybeth hadn't even thought of that. What if she got stuck in a cabin full of strangers?

She almost groaned again.

"One of the purposes of camp is to let you get acquainted with other girls," Sister Jackson said, "so very likely you won't all be together."

Marybeth was pleased to see that the other Bee Theres looked as alarmed as she felt.

"However," Sister Jackson went on, "I'm sure the camp leaders will assign at least two of you together."

"But there are five of us," wailed Elena. "So that leaves one of us alone with strangers."

Now everybody groaned. They all looked at one another as if wondering who that unlucky person would be.

Sister Jackson held up her hand. "Now what did I say? At least two of you will be assigned together. That means very likely the other three will be assigned to the same cabin. There are seven girls in each cabin, plus a CIT."

"Kit?" Sunshine repeated.

"It's spelled C-I-T," Sister Jackson said. "Counselor in training. She's always an older girl who has been to camp before. She'll help you with all the things you'll be doing."

That sounded better.

Becca glanced around at the rest of the class. "Who's up for a day at the mall tomorrow? I need some new white shorts and a couple of camp shirts."

Before anyone could answer, Sister Jackson said, "I wouldn't advise new clothes. Wear your grubbies. You'll be way out in the mountains."

Marybeth wished she hadn't said that.

"It will be dirty, and besides, there won't be any boys to dress up for. The ones who'll be there helping in the kitchen are just trees. Remember?"

Marybeth would never be able to think of Sam as a tree. But maybe she'd better get used to it, since he wasn't talking to her anyway.

"You're going to love girls camp," Sister Jackson said.

"As long as we have someone we know in our cabin," Elena whispered.

Marybeth wouldn't have thought Elena would be the one to worry about being in a cabin with strangers. Elena wasn't afraid of getting up and singing in front of a whole room full of strangers.

Sister Jackson was still talking. "During the day you'll be spending most of your time on certification, but at night we play. The first night we'll have a big bonfire get-acquainted rally and a sing-along. We'll have games and contests the second night, and Wednesday is skit night. On Thursday night the bishops from all the wards will come up, and the best skits will be presented for them. Friday morning will be the testimony meeting, and then we'll come home."

It did sound fun, if it weren't for the dark hours in between.

"We must get on to the lesson now," Sister Jackson said. "It's on self-mastery today."

Marybeth ducked her head. Had Sister Jackson's X-ray eyes been looking right inside her again? Had she seen that Marybeth needed to master her fear of the dark?

When the class was over, what Marybeth found herself thinking about was choice and accountability. Choice and accountability.

There was still a very slim chance that she might get out of going to girls camp if she did things right. Or actually, if she did them wrong. Choice and accountability. If Marybeth chose to give a talk in sacrament meeting next week that would embarrass her whole family, she would have to suffer the consequences. Dad would make her accountable for it and would probably ground her for the following week. She'd have to stay home from camp. She'd miss out on being a part of all the experiences that the other Bee Theres would come home telling about. But after her experiment with the night light, she wasn't sure which scenario was worse.

The days passed quickly. Dad and Mom went with Randy to the temple, a mystery to Marybeth. People went there to get married, but Randy wasn't getting married. He was taking out his endowments, Mom said, but Marybeth didn't see anything that looked like endowments when Randy came home. She'd find out more about it someday. If she lived through girls camp, that is.

Then it was Sunday again. The day of Randy's farewell. The day before girls camp started.

Marybeth had prepared a talk that would embarrass her family. Forget self-mastery. She was going to get out of going to girls camp if there was still a possibility. Dad would for sure ground her if she gave that talk.

She had an alternate talk prepared too, just in case. Just in case she decided she couldn't face the accountability part if she gave the first one. She was getting cold feet. Dad might worse than ground her if she did what she'd planned. He might check her into the psychiatric unit at the hospital where he worked. He might send her off to live with her Aunt Milda, who lived on a farm in Wyoming, seventy miles from the nearest town. It was probably darker there than at girls camp.

Downstairs Dad started hollering that they all had to come right now or they'd be late.

Marybeth chickened out. She threw the embarrassing talk into her wastebasket and shoved the other one into the pocket of her best flowered skirt.

The program was all printed up and the Scouts were handing it out at the door as people arrived. Marybeth examined her copy as she and the rest of her family walked down the aisle to the podium, where they were all supposed to sit. The twins were scheduled to speak first. They'd probably made a bargain that if they spoke at all, they had to be first and get it over with.

Katie was next, then Marybeth, then Darla.

There was to be a musical number by a quartet of Randy's friends singing "Ye Elders of Israel." Then Mom would speak, followed by Dad. Then Randy, who was listed as Elder Randall V. Stewart. V for

Vincent. Marybeth had almost forgotten that his middle name was Vincent.

The final talk would be by the bishop, and the closing hymn would be "God Be With You Till We Meet Again."

The meeting began with the opening hymn and the invocation, followed by the announcements given by the bishop.

Two guys from the priests quorum blessed the sacrament, and Garth and Grant helped to pass the bread and water to the congregation. Their hands shook so much that Marybeth was surprised they didn't drop the trays.

When they'd returned the trays to the table and the priests had spread the snowy cloth over them, Garth and Grant trembled their way up onto the podium. Grant collapsed into a seat while Garth found his way to the pulpit.

Marybeth wasn't sure what he said. He kept his head down as he read from a computer sheet that rattled in his hand as if there were a high wind. Finally he mumbled, "Name-Je-Chri-men."

Marybeth wondered what Sister Jackson would have done with his deacons class. She remembered how Sister Jackson had shaped up the Beehive class, making them "articulate" their prayers and talks so that they could be understood. She'd made them say

"In the name of Jesus Christ, amen," over and over again so they'd never forget not to mumble.

Grant was just as bad. His talk wasn't even as long as Garth's. He tottered as he returned to his seat, and Marybeth figured he'd cut it short rather than risk fainting right there in front of everybody.

Both boys slid far down in their seats, and even from where she sat, Marybeth could feel the heat from their frightened bodies.

Katie was next. She didn't show the slightest fear. She stood in the pulpit without even any notes, and she told what a great brother Randy was. She told about several things that made him special, and she ended saying that every kid he met would join the church just to be with him.

As she finished, Marybeth pulled her talk from her pocket, glad she'd decided not to do the goofy one. Garth and Grant had done enough to embarrass the family. She wanted to continue on with the spirit Katie had brought to the meeting.

She spread her sheets of paper on the pulpit and began reading. "Our family is so big . . . " Oh, no. She'd brought the embarrassing talk! How had she got them mixed up?

Frantically she felt in her pocket for the good talk, the one that would tell how much she loved Randy, how much she would miss him, what a terrific big brother he was.

It wasn't there. She remembered she'd thrown something into her wastebasket just before leaving her room. She'd thrown away the wrong one.

She'd have to ad lib.

She couldn't think of a single word.

She looked back down at her papers. "Our family is so big," she squeaked, "that my dad had to take out a kennel license."

There was a ripple of laughter from the congregation.

"There are ten of us," she said, "counting our parents. Every now and then Dad tries to give one of us to the church for tithing."

Another laugh, this time bigger.

"But the bishop always gives us back, saying he can't drop us through the night deposit slot at the bank."

Behind her Marybeth heard the bishop laugh.

She swallowed. She didn't dare look up, and there was no way she was going to look at her family behind her. She was just going to have to stumble on to the end, unless somebody stabbed her with the music director's baton before she finished.

"You know my dad's a psychiatrist," she said. "He makes money using other people's heads."

More laughter.

Doggedly Marybeth continued. "My mom is pretty clever. She crossed a can of alphabet soup with flour and made mongrammed pancakes. She admits that she's approaching forty, but she won't tell us from which direction. And then there's Randy."

She paused to take a deep breath and let the laughter die down.

"I just don't know what kind of a missionary he'll make. Do you know that he saves burned-out light bulbs to use in his darkroom? He takes a yardstick to bed to see how long he sleeps. He uses two hands to brush his teeth. He holds the toothbrush with one hand and uses the other one to push his head back and forth."

Behind her, Randy hooted with laughter.

Marybeth hurried on to tell about Garth and Grant, who had such big feet they had to pull their pants on over their heads. And about Darla, who was so thin that if she stood sideways her teacher marked her absent.

There was still more writing on the page, but Marybeth decided she'd said enough. The bishop had probably sneaked out to his office to call Salt Lake and tell them to excommunicate her immediately for being too frivolous at a missionary farewell.

"So you can see why Randy wants to go on a mission," she finished. "Just to get away from his family."

She scarcely heard the rest of the meeting. Darla told about how when she was eight and going to be baptized, Randy had convinced her that she needed some sins to be washed away. "He told me," she said, "that Mama didn't wash clean clothes and so I couldn't be baptized if I hadn't done any sins. So he got me to steal a giant zucchini from Brother Turvey's garden."

Darla paused to let people laugh, but they didn't laugh as loud as they did when Marybeth spoke.

"Mama caught us with it, and after she talked to Brother Turvey, she cooked it and made us eat the whole thing."

Mom and Dad both talked about the adventure of raising eight children and how sometimes they weren't fit to inflict on the world, but each one grew up to be a right decent human being, and they were proud to send them on missions.

Randy gave a nice talk about how he'd looked forward to this day all of his life.

The meeting finally ended. Marybeth tried to escape, but Katie wrapped her arms around her waist. "You didn't tell anything about me," she said. "You should have said something about me."

Dad caught Marybeth's arm, and she wondered if

he was going to deck her right there in front of everybody. Pulling her to him, he gave her a hug. "I didn't realize you were the family comedian," he said, laughing.

The bishop shook her hand and said he hadn't laughed so hard in a long time. Other people came up to say how much they'd enjoyed her talk.

And Sister Jackson said, "I'm going to recommend you to be the mistress of ceremonies on Thursday night when all the bishops come to camp."

Morosely, Marybeth waited to go home. Her last hope had failed.

She had to pack for girls camp.

CHAPTER
12

All campers were supposed to meet at the stake center parking lot at 10:30 on Monday morning for what was listed on the instruction sheet as a "brown-bag brunch." Marybeth lay awake most of Sunday night, hoping there'd be a major earthquake, or that Hurricane What's-its-name would blow up from Mexico, or that a previously unknown volcano would erupt within two miles of her home. Or maybe she could come down with chicken pox or measles or some other ugly-looking disease.

Anything would be better than going off to an event where you were seriously certain of losing your total self-esteem.

But Marybeth woke up perfectly healthy, and the morning was bright and clear and hot. There was a little smog, but that was all the more reason to go to the mountains.

Marybeth sighed, then showered and got dressed. Hoisting her duffel to her shoulder, she went downstairs, heading bravely into her inevitable fate.

Dad was just leaving for work. He kissed Darla and Marybeth goodbye and didn't offer any last minute instructions on how to behave.

Mom made them swallow some cereal and orange juice before she released them to Randy, who had volunteered to drop them off at the church on his way to his last day of work.

After the goodbyes were said, they drove off in Randy's rattly old car. The last thing Marybeth saw out of the car's rear window was Mom climbing up into the tree again.

Chaos was the only word that could describe what was going on in the church parking lot. More than a hundred girls from the eight wards in the stake milled around, herded this way and that by perspiring camp directors and Young Women leaders.

"Isn't this *fun?*" Sunshine exclaimed when she saw Marybeth. "We're actually going to camp. Aren't you excited?"

"Yeah." Marybeth tried to sound excited. Darla had disappeared with some older girls, and Marybeth doubted that she'd see her again that day.

"There's Becca and Elena." Sunshine jumped up and down, waving both arms in the air.

Marybeth looked around for Carlie but didn't see her. Maybe the volcano had erupted near *her* house by mistake. Or maybe *she* had come down with measles.

A loudspeaker crackled. "Dump your duffels over by the palm tree," said a voice whose owner wasn't even in sight. "The truck is ready to load them."

Marybeth and Sunshine headed toward the rapidly growing pile. Becca and Elena joined them.

"Isn't this fun?" Sunshine said.

Then Carlie was there too, and Sunshine repeated, "Isn't this fun?"

Marybeth wanted to ask if she knew any other words, but she didn't say it. It wasn't Sunshine's fault that Marybeth's life was about to go down the drain.

The loudspeaker crackled again. "Everybody form a line and go inside, please. There are three tables in the foyer, where you'll get your cabin assignments."

The next words couldn't be heard because all the girls started talking about whom they wanted as their cabin mates.

"Quiet," screeched the loudspeaker. "Please," it said in calmer tones. "All those with last names starting with A through G go to table number one. H through P to table number two. Everybody else to table number three. After you have your assignment and your name badge, get your brown-bag brunch from the counter outside the kitchen, then go to the cultural hall and look for a pole with your cabin number on it. Go there to eat."

The chaos got worse.

It was going to take all day just to get past those tables. There wouldn't be time to get to Cougar Camp way up there in the mountains, and they'd all be sent home to sleep that night.

But before long everybody was in a line that snaked back out into the parking lot, and the line was actually moving. It moved quite fast.

Marybeth was assigned to Cabin 13. Well, that figured. Actually, it kind of had possibilities. She wasn't too unhappy about it.

Becca was assigned to that cabin too. Carlie, Elena, and Sunshine were to be in Cabin 5, not even close to number 13.

But that was all right. Maybe they'd be far enough away so they couldn't hear Marybeth's shrieks of terror during the night.

She and Becca peeked into their brown bags as they made their way toward the pole that read "13." There was a toasted English muffin inside, plus a couple pieces of cheese, an apple, and a small carton of milk.

Sister Jackson was standing alongside the Cabin 13 pole. She looked as perfect as ever, dressed in blue jeans that looked as if they'd just been ironed and a blue and white striped shirt. Her hair was starched to stiff perfection, as always.

"Are you in our our cabin?" Becca asked, and when Sister Jackson nodded, Becca exclaimed, "Good-o!"

"Of course the cabin CIT will be in charge of things," Sister Jackson said. "I'll just be there as sort of a chaperon."

Marybeth wasn't sure how she felt about that. On one hand, it was nice to have somebody she knew as her adult leader. On the other hand, she hated to have Sister Jackson see her when she became a whimpering vegetable in the middle of the dark night.

Sister Jackson was introducing everybody. "This is DeeDee," she said, pointing to an older girl. "She's our cabin CIT."

Marybeth's mind stumbled over that one until she remembered that CIT meant counselor-in-training.

DeeDee was blond and cute and looked like a cheerleader. She didn't look like someone who'd understand how a person could be afraid of the dark.

Marybeth knew two of the other girls assigned to her cabin. There was a girl named Celeste from Second Ward and one named Lauren from South

Ward. She'd seen the other two, Rosaline and Petra, at a stake conference or somewhere.

DeeDee was pasting black gummi worms to the foreheads of everyone in her cabin. "This is just to tell everybody we're from Cabin 13," she said. "Let's hear it for Cabin 13!"

"Yay, yay, Cabin 13," Petra yelled, and then all the others yelled it.

There were other groups yelling, all over the cultural hall. It was kind of exciting, especially when Marybeth noticed that nobody else had a cabin identification nearly as neat as the black gummi worms on their foreheads. The girls in cabin 12, right next to them, had bright flowered bands around their foreheads, and the girls in Cabin 14 on the other side had butterfly clips in their hair.

Petra jittered around just the way Sunshine had done. "Isn't this fun?" she said.

And Marybeth finally had to admit it was.

"Everybody quiet now!" the loudspeaker yelled. "We'll have the blessing on the food and a prayer for our safety. As soon as we eat, we'll be off!"

Marybeth cheered right along with the others.

All of the Bee Theres were assigned to the same bus. They sat together, Becca and Marybeth on one side, Sunshine and Elena on the other side, and Carlie on the seat right in front of them with Petra.

They hadn't finished eating by the time the bus was ready to go, so most of the girls still had their brown-bag brunches. Marybeth continued to eat, wondering if the motion of the bus would make her sick and they would send her home. She sort of hoped it would, but then again she hoped it wouldn't.

The bus had no sooner started rolling than a girl stood up and yelled, "Let's sing 'Purple Toe!'" She had a name tag that said her name was Jana.

"I don't know that song," Carlie said.

A girl in front of her said, "Don't worry. You soon will. We made it up last year."

All those who knew it sang, *"Jana has a purple toe."*

Another girl stood up and yelled, *"Don't you know?"*

Then everybody sang, *"Purple toe, don't you know? Jana has a purple toe, and we all love it so."*

Another girl with a name tag that read Heather stood up and, pointing to her mouth, said, "Achy tooth."

Everybody sang, *"Heather has an achy tooth."*

Somebody leaped up and said, *"That's the truth."*

Then everybody said, *"Achy tooth, that's the truth. Heather has an achy tooth, and we all love it so."*

"See," the girl in front of Carlie said, "someone says something, then you have to rhyme the next line with that and just finish it off. Get it?"

Marybeth got it. When she nodded, Becca poked her. "Say something," she urged.

The only thing Marybeth could think of was what she held in her hand. She jumped up. "Piece of toast," she yelled.

Girls looked around to see her name tag, then sang, *"Marybeth has a piece of toast."*

"See a ghost!" somebody yelled.

The girls picked it up. *"Piece of toast, see a ghost, Marybeth has a piece of toast, and we all love it so."*

Marybeth sank down into her seat. Cabin 13. Ghost.

Would she survive this week?

CHAPTER
13

The mountain roads were steep, and the bus swayed as it went around the curves. Petra, who sat with Carlie on the seat in front of Marybeth and Becca, put her hands over her eyes. She looked pale, which made the black gummi worm glued to her forehead look big and a little menacing.

Marybeth reached up to touch her shoulder. "What's the matter, Petra?"

Petra opened her hands enough to peer out at Marybeth. "It's embarrassing," she whispered, "but I'm afraid of roads like this. I keep thinking we're going to fall off the edge."

"We won't fall off," Marybeth assured her. "Look, the road is wide."

Just then a truck came the other way and the bus had to go over close to the outer edge of the road.

Petra whimpered. Marybeth looked down, down, down into a rocky ravine. She wasn't afraid.

"We have a really good driver," she told Petra. "He won't run off the road."

"A bus went off the road last year," Petra whispered. "I saw it on TV. I'm scared." She clamped her hands tight over her eyes again. "I feel so stupid," she moaned.

Marybeth knew all about fear and how stupid it made a person feel. "Let's sing `Purple Toe' again," she said. "You be first, Petra."

Petra drew a long breath, like a shudder. Lowering her hands a little, she pointed her forefingers at her reddened eyes and said, "Ketchup eyes."

"Petra has two ketchup eyes," Marybeth sang, nudging Becca and Carlie to join her.

"Bring french fries," yelled Sunshine from across the aisle.

"Ketchup eyes, bring french fries," everybody sang. *"Petra has two ketchup eyes, and we all love her so."*

Petra giggled. She poked Carlie. "It's your turn."

Carlie picked it right up. Grabbing her earlobes she said, "Spandex ears."

Everybody sang, *"Carlie has two Spandex ears."*

"Bought at Sears," someone shouted, and everybody sang, *"Spandex ears, bought at Sears. Carlie has two Spandex ears, and we all love them so."*

Petra took her hands completely away from her face and laughed along with the others. "Thanks," she whispered to Marybeth as the laughter died away. "You're really brave."

Marybeth shook her head. Her own fear was far more embarrassing that Petra's. In fact, Petra might not even want her for a friend once she found Marybeth was afraid of the dark.

Marybeth looked around fearfully as the bus at last lumbered into the clearing in front of the Camp Cougar cabins. The pine trees that crowded so close to the cabins were even taller and more gloomy than she'd imagined. They seemed to be waiting for her, almost bending down to take a look at her. Late afternoon shadows, dark and shapeless, hung in their needled branches.

"Everybody out," yelled the stake camp director, who was on Marybeth's bus. "Look for your cabin CITs. They'll be holding up paper plates with the cabin numbers on them."

The girls scrambled to get out of the bus. Becca was the first one to spot DeeDee, Cabin 13's CIT. DeeDee had made a skeleton face on her paper plate, with a big 1 in one vacant eye socket and a 3 in the other.

She motioned for her girls to come to her. "Come get your cabin badges," she yelled.

Marybeth, Becca, and Petra hurried over to her, along with Celeste, Lauren, and Rosaline, who'd been at the back of the bus.

DeeDee handed each girl a Milk Bone, the kind you feed to dogs. They were painted white and were suspended from a large safety pin. Each girl's name was written on one, in wavery, ghosty printing.

"These are your ID badges," she said. "Pin them on your shirt each morning. They'll let everybody know you're from Cabin 13."

She pointed toward one of the cabins that stood back in the dark trees a little way. Marybeth saw that a plastic skeleton hung beside the doorway.

She looked around at some of the other cabins. One had a unicorn by its door, and another had an enormous sunflower. Cabin 5 sported a tall cardboard figure of a girl in an evening dress with a crown on her head. A banner that crossed her body from shoulder to hip declared "Miss Galaxy."

"Wow," Marybeth murmured. "Lucky Carlie and Sunshine and Elena. They get to be beauty queens."

"I'd rather be a skeleton in Cabin 13," Becca said cheerfully.

"So would I," Petra said.

She certainly seemed to be all over her earlier fear.

Across the clearing Marybeth saw a truck stop

near a long, low building. Quincy and Sam climbed out of it. Sam looked all around the clearing as if he were searching for something. Or somebody.

Marybeth's heart skipped a beat. Was he looking for *her?*

A lot of the other girls must have seen the guys, because there were some sighs and a couple of whistles. The camp director immediately turned on her loudspeaker.

"They're just trees, girls," she said. "Remember that. Any men around camp are just trees."

The girls groaned.

Marybeth was glad the camp director had said that. She didn't want to be competing with all those other girls for Sam's attention.

"And while I'm at it," the camp director continued, "I might as well remind you of all the forbidden M's. Men, mirrors, and make-up. The men are trees, and if you brought mirrors and make-up with you, leave them in your duffels. We're not going to worry about those things while we're here. And no hair dryers or hot curlers. We're all going to be totally natural while we're here at camp."

Marybeth hadn't brought any of those things with her anyway. Sister Jackson had told her class to leave all that stuff at home.

Marybeth was suddenly glad that she *couldn't* talk

to Sam there at camp. She didn't want him to see her too natural.

"All right, everybody." This was the activities director now. "Everybody go to your cabins and get unpacked so you can go to the dining hall for dinner. After you've eaten, we'll have a sing-along around the campfire."

It didn't take Marybeth and the other girls in Cabin 13 long to unpack. All they had with them was a change of clothes or two, which they hung on hooks next to their beds.

The cabin wasn't as bad as Marybeth had expected. Each building was shaped like a plus sign, with four cabins sticking out from a central shower area. Each cabin had an outside door and another door leading into the central area.

Cabin 13 was the north leg of the plus sign, so it would be the darkest, which didn't please Marybeth too much. Otherwise, it wasn't too bad.

There were four bunk beds, and she got one of the upper bunks. She was pleased about that. It meant she would be farther away from creepy things that might show up.

"Okay, you guys," DeeDee said. "Our theme song is going to be the one about 'Did you ever see a hearse pass by and think that you were the next to die.'"

Everybody knew that one. It was so gross.

"I love it," Petra said.

Marybeth was surprised. She didn't seem like the same girl who'd been whimpering about the scary ride up the mountain.

"We'll be singing it tonight when each cabin has a turn at the campfire," DeeDee said. "Let's run through it a couple of times, just for practice."

While they sang the gruesome song, DeeDee went around and pasted outlines of white skeleton heads on the two windows.

The last thing she did before they went to dinner was draw grinning skeleton teeth around each girl's mouth and fill in around their eyes with black eyebrow pencil, making them look as if their eyesockets were hollow.

"I thought we weren't supposed to wear make-up," Becca said, as she had her face painted.

"Only for costuming," DeeDee said.

Petra grinned as she watched. "Way to go," she said.

Marybeth was a little self-conscious about going to dinner looking like they did, but she found that girls in some of the other cabins had done things just as weird. The girls from Cabin 9 all had shaving cream in their hair, which made it possible for them to create all kinds of hairdos. The girls in Cabin 5, the Miss

Galaxy cabin, had put balloons under their T-shirts so that they seemed to have enormous bosoms. Everybody from Cabin 3 had a set of huge wax lips, which they had to take off to eat.

It was fun. Even Marybeth had to admit to herself that she was glad she hadn't missed all this.

The sing-along was fun too, except for the darkness in the trees behind the girls. Each cabin had some kind of song to sing. Cabin 13 was a great hit with its hearse song.

Then it was time for the evening prayer and bed.

That was the time Marybeth had been dreading, when the lights were turned out and the darkness smothered them.

After she'd climbed up to her narrow upper bunk, she checked to see that her little flashlight was on the beam above her bed where she'd put it, then squeezed her eyes shut. She assured herself that if she didn't open them, she could imagine that the cabin was well lighted.

It worked quite well. Even while they all talked after getting in bed, she didn't open her eyes. It worked so well that she actually went to sleep.

She didn't know how long she slept, but she was awakened by the squeak of the outside door opening.

She sat up, whamming her head on the overhead

beam, and strained to see in the darkness. Had the squeak been her imagination?

She couldn't remember where she'd put her flashlight.

She couldn't hear any footsteps or anything like that. The others must not have heard the door opening, because nobody else seemed to be awake.

Marybeth was ready to squeeze her eyes shut again and lie down when suddenly she saw it. A white, luminous ghost with huge black eye sockets there below her.

Then, to her total horror, it began to rise, floating slowly, slowly up toward her bunk.

All of her very worst fears had come true. This was worse than the ghost at the old farmhouse.

Marybeth tried to scream, but all she could do was make a raspy gasping sound and shake the bed, hoping to wake Becca, who slept below her.

CHAPTER
14

Apparently Becca woke up because Marybeth heard her say, "Hey, we're having an earthquake."

Then she screamed.

Marybeth didn't know whether Becca was screaming because her bed was shaking or because she'd seen the slowly rising ghost. But at least she'd awakened the others.

From the upper bunk across the room Celeste yelled, "Ghost! Ghost! Ghost!" Her voice sounded ragged and hoarse.

Below her, Rosaline screamed wordlessly.

Even DeeDee, their CIT, was yelling. "It's okay, girls," she hollered. "Get your flashlights."

There was a lot of thumping as everybody searched for flashlights. Marybeth felt under her pillow for hers, trying to remember where she'd put it.

She was trying to scream, but nothing would come out of her throat. It was closed tight with total terror. All she could do was crouch there making small gasping sounds.

Sister Jackson, who'd been snoring softly just a few seconds before, woke up and turned on her flashlight.

"Stay calm, girls," she said. "I'm sure it's only a prank."

She shone her flashlight at the ghost.

It wasn't a ghost at all. It was just a big white balloon with something like tissue paper trailing from it.

"Who did this?" demanded Rosaline. In the dim light Marybeth could see her eyes peering over the top of her sleeping bag.

Other flashlights went on. DeeDee got up and switched on the overhead light.

There was a giggle just outside the door. Someone opened it, and then Petra came in, grinning guiltily.

"It was too good to pass up," she said. "You know, Cabin 13 and all our ghost decorations. I had to add a little to it."

Everybody groaned, and Rosaline threw her pillow at Petra.

"Well, you almost scared the hair off my head," Celeste said. She didn't sound very angry, though.

Petra giggled again. "I guess I got everybody

going. Except Marybeth. She's up there cool as a cucumber. She's not afraid of *anything.*"

Everybody turned to look at Marybeth, who still couldn't say a word. She waved to them.

Cool as a cucumber, was she? Couldn't they tell how she was still rigid with fright?

It was the worst experience she'd had since the ghost had appeared at the old historical farm. She knew she wasn't going to sleep a wink the rest of the night. Not in a dark cabin with more darkness pushing in from outside, shaped by the skeleton heads DeeDee had put on the windows.

"Not a peep out of her," Rosaline was saying, looking admiringly up at Marybeth. "How did you keep from screaming, Marybeth?"

Marybeth couldn't speak, so she shrugged.

"She's never afraid of anything," Becca said. Even she looked impressed by the fact that Marybeth was so cool in this situation.

Marybeth gave her a shaky grin, glad that she'd never let on to the other Bee Theres how scared she'd been at the old historical farm.

DeeDee glanced at Sister Jackson as if to ask who was in charge here. Sister Jackson made a motion with her hand that said DeeDee was.

"We need to get to sleep," DeeDee said. "The light is on all night in the shower room. We'll leave the door leading in there open just a little in case anybody else gets ghost ideas."

Oh, thank you, thank you, Marybeth thought. But she still couldn't say a word.

She thought she wouldn't sleep at all that night. There was too much going through her mind. Maybe she should just tell the other girls in the cabin how terrified she'd been. They had all been scared by the "ghost." It wouldn't be any disgrace to admit she'd been frightened too.

But how could she do that now that they'd made such a big thing of how brave she was? That would make her seem wimpier than ever for not confessing right on the spot that she had been too frightened even to speak.

No, she'd just have to try to live up to her new image.

Outside she heard the wind whispering in the dark pines, and far away she heard the faint rumble of thunder. No, she wouldn't be sleeping at all. She dragged her heavy eyelids open to make sure the door really was open, letting in light from the shower room.

The next thing she knew it was morning and the other girls were chattering as they got dressed.

"That was fun last night, Petra," Rosaline said.

Fun?

"You girls will have the best prank of the night to tell about, I think," DeeDee said.

Marybeth sat up in her bunk, whacking her head again on the beam above her. "Do you mean people play pranks all the time?" she asked, rubbing the sore spot on her head. "Every night?"

"Maybe." DeeDee seemed nonchalant about it. "But there's a rule against anything that might hurt somebody or damage any property."

Privately Marybeth thought there should have been a rule about ghosts. The prank last night could have given her a heart attack.

But it hadn't, and she felt quite happy this morning. There was a whole day before it got dark again.

The daylight showing through the skeleton heads was a little gray and gloomy. Marybeth remembered the thunder the night before.

Rosaline opened the door and looked out. "Do you think it's going to lightning?" She sounded worried.

"Maybe," Marybeth said. "But it won't hurt us."

Rosaline didn't seem convinced. "Are you sure?"

Before Marybeth could answer, a bunch of girls outside started singing, *"Norman, you are a big fat snake. Norman, can you be real or fake? Norman, come be a Mormon. Come join us, Norman, our Camp Cougar snake."*

Petra ran to the door. "Has somebody seen Norman?" she yelled.

"No," someone answered. "We're inviting him to show up."

Laughing, Petra ran outside. "Come on, everybody," she called back to her cabin mates.

"I have to comb my hair," wailed Celeste.

"Forget it," DeeDee said. "Today might be the bad-hair contest. Let's go."

All of the girls hurried toward the door.

"Come on, Sister Jackson." DeeDee waited by the door. "Don't want to be late for breakfast."

Sister Jackson was standing by her bed, digging in the duffel she'd brought with her. "You girls go," she said. "I'll be there in a minute."

DeeDee joined the others, and they all headed for the dining hall. Girls came from every part of the camp. Some were wearing bright-colored headbands; others had neckerchiefs to identify which cabin they came from.

Marybeth's cabin mates all had their dog-bone name badges pinned to their camp shirts.

All but her. "I forgot my bone badge," she said, turning back. "Save me a place at the table, Becca."

Sister Jackson was still standing by her bed when Marybeth got back to the cabin. She was looking at something she held in her hand. Probably a picture of Brother Turvey.

"I guess you miss him, don't you?" Marybeth asked gently as she scrambled up to her bunk and found her bone badge where she'd stashed it on the overhead beam. Her flashlight was there too. She remembered now that she'd put it there.

"Yes," Sister Jackson said. "I do miss him."

"I guess you'll be getting married soon." Marybeth was glad now that Sister Jackson and Brother Turvey hadn't got married during camp week as she'd hoped earlier that they would. She was beginning to enjoy it here.

Sister Jackson was looking puzzled. "Married?"

Marybeth nodded. "You and Brother Turvey."

Sister Jackson laughed. "Marybeth, look." She held up the picture that was in her hand. It wasn't Brother Turvey.

"This was my husband," she said. "Today would have been our forty-fifth wedding anniversary if he'd lived." She put the picture down. "Now what's this about Brother Turvey?"

Marybeth felt foolish. "Well, y'know, you and him, y'know, being in love and all. We . . . I just thought, y'know, that maybe you'd be getting married soon." She was falling back into her old habit of saying "y'know" every few words. Too bad Grant wasn't there to yip as a reminder.

Sister Jackson smiled. "Brother Turvey and I are very good friends. But as for getting married . . . I'll confess something to you, Marybeth. I'd be afraid to get married again. You girls would probably call me chicken, but I couldn't face loving someone again and taking the chance of losing him. There won't be any wedding." She patted her perfect hair, which certainly wouldn't win any prizes on bad-hair day. "And now, fellow camper, we'd better go to breakfast."

As they hurried toward the dining hall, Marybeth marveled that Sister Jackson would be afraid of anything, especially of love. Afraid of *love*, for heaven's sake. She couldn't wait to tell the other girls.

No, she wouldn't tell them. It would be a secret between her and Sister Jackson.

The contest that morning was not for bad hair but for which cabin's campers had got the least sleep. That gave Cabin 13 the chance to tell about their ghost. They didn't win the prize, which was a bag of peanut M&M's, but everybody laughed about the ghost. The prize went to Cabin 9, whose campers had been awake most of the night talking about what kind of dates they liked best. Those who weren't sixteen yet told what kind they hoped for. One girl said she didn't care, as long as the guy was alive and breathing.

After breakfast, all campers were instructed to return to their cabins long enough to write to their parents so that a letter would have time to get to their homes before they returned. Dark clouds were gathering outside, so the girls in Cabin 13 turned on their light, which drove the dark shadows away.

Marybeth dug out the paper and pen they'd all been instructed to bring, but she couldn't think of anything to say. The cabin was noisy with the other campers laughing and talking about what they were going to write. Writing letters wasn't Marybeth's thing, especially when there was a lot of noise. She didn't especially like to write anything. Maybe she could concentrate better if she went outside and got away from the others. Maybe she'd even climb up in a tree.

She thought of her mom climbing up into the tree each day. Did she go there to get away from the noise and confusion that was part of their house on any day? But there was more to it than that. It was still a puzzle.

Marybeth bit the end of her pen as she listened to the scratching sounds the others made writing their letters. They were saying *something* to their parents.

She couldn't think of what to write. Maybe about the ghost?

Then Petra slid something over to her. "My sister gave me this," she said. "She got it when she went to camp. Just copy it and fill in the blanks with whatever names you want."

Marybeth read the letter and immediately began copying it. It would be a great joke.

She giggled softly as she wrote:

Dear Mom and Dad and Family,

I am having a great time at Camp Cougar. Sister Jackson said we should write to you in case you saw the flood on TV and got worried. We are all okay except for Sunshine, who got washed away along with all our sleeping bags. We really wondered how we were going to sleep tonight. But we found the bags all right.

Becca had been reading over her shoulder, and now she too began copying the letter, snickering as she scribbled. Marybeth continued writing:

None of the rest of us were in the flood because we were up on the mountain looking for Becca when it happened. You might call her parents and tell them she's okay. She can't write because of the cast. Sister Jackson is mad at her for going on a hike alone without telling her. Becca did tell her, but Sister Jackson didn't hear her because of the fire. Did you know that if you pour white gas on a fire, the gas can might blow up? Carlie will look okay once her hair and eyebrows grow back again. It's time to go now. We're going to work on our First Aid certification this morning. Isn't it nice that we can practice on Elena's arm? The bleeding has slowed down enough now so we can tell where to put the tourniquet.

Don't worry about me. I threw up all night, but Sister Jackson said it is probably just food poisoning.

Love,

Marybeth

P.S. Oh yes, we found Sunshine all right. We hung her upside down in the dining hall. She'll be okay once all the floodwater drains out.

Marybeth laughed as she folded the letter and put it inside the envelope. She wished she could be home when her family read it. Even Garth and Grant would probably like it.

The day passed quickly, with storm clouds gathering overhead and dripping a few drops of rain as the Beehives worked on certifying in woods lore. There were darker clouds in the west, and it looked as if there really would be lightning, as Rosaline feared.

Marybeth wasn't afraid of lightning, but she was afraid of those threatening clouds that would make the darkness tonight more intense. Even now there were black shadows in the trees.

But night was still a few hours away.

It was when everybody was heading toward the dining hall for lunch that Marybeth saw Sam. He was crossing the bonfire area, heading for the kitchen. He had a leafy branch stuck down the back of his T-shirt and some leaves around his neck.

"Hi, tree," Marybeth said. The camp rules had said you should think of any guys as trees, but they didn't say you couldn't talk to the trees.

Sam grinned as if he was glad to see a familiar face. He opened his mouth, but before he said anything, they heard somebody screech, "Snake! Snake!"

Snake? Norman, maybe? The giant gold and green snake that had terrorized campers for years?

A dozen girls were shrieking now. "Snake! Snake!"

"We'd better check this out," Marybeth said to Sam. "I wouldn't want to miss a chance to meet Norman."

She ran toward the edge of the clearing where most of the screaming was going on.

"Is it Norman?" she asked one girl who ran past her.

"He didn't mention his name," the girl gasped as she scampered toward the dining hall.

"Where is he?" Marybeth asked another girl.

The girl merely pointed behind her as she ran.

Marybeth hurried to where two tense but curious girls stood looking down at a slender, foot-long garter

156

snake. An innocent, harmless little garter snake. Marybeth was well acquainted with that variety. They'd even been talking about them earlier in their woods-lore discussion.

"Well, Norman," she said, bending over him. "You're not nearly as fearsome as everybody said you'd be." He flicked his little forked tongue at her.

The two watching girls giggled nervously.

"Mind if we borrow you for a while?" Marybeth picked up the snake. "We'll use you this afternoon to show what kind of snakes not to be afraid of. Then we'll let you go."

"Eeeee-yu," one of the watching girls said. "Aren't you afraid of him?"

"She's the girl who's not afraid of anything," the other girl said. "Petra told me."

Her reputation must be spreading.

"Sam, come look at his." Marybeth looked for him.

He wasn't there. He still stood back where he and Marybeth had met. He watched her with horror on his face.

She remembered then how he'd acted after Garth and Grant had told him the tales about Norman, the giant snake. He'd torn off his snake stick-on tattoo. He'd seemed embarrassed to even face her when she'd asked him what he thought of Norman.

He was afraid. Afraid of snakes.

He looked at her now, plainly understanding that she knew of his fear. He was probably wondering if she'd tell.

She smiled at him and lowered the wriggling snake so he wouldn't have to look at it.

No, she wouldn't tell. That was another secret she'd keep.

She understood fear.

And there were three more nights to live through. Eventually some of the campers were sure to discover her own secret. She hoped they would be kind enough not to tell everybody what it was.

CHAPTER
15

The dark clouds continued to pile up above the tree-tops all afternoon. Marybeth saw Rosaline looking anxiously at them every now and then.

The stake camp director reported that she'd tuned in on a radio weather report that said the storm would blow over that night, leaving them with sunny skies the rest of the week. But that didn't seem to comfort Rosaline much.

Marybeth wanted to tell her that they'd be okay, that they'd be safe in the cabins during any thunder and lightning. They could leave the lights on, and that would keep the darkness away.

But it wasn't darkness that Rosaline feared. No, that was Marybeth's own private fear. That was what *she* was worried about. She didn't say anything to

Rosaline, who might be just as embarrassed about being afraid as Marybeth was.

Besides, maybe the storm wouldn't be that bad.

After some free time, there was an announcement that the girls from each ward should get together to rehearse their skits. The girls from Marybeth's ward were supposed to meet in a small clearing behind Cabins 5, 6, 7, and 8.

It was the first time Marybeth had seen her sister Darla since they'd arrived.

"How's it going, Twerp?" Darla asked as all the girls were coming to the clearing. "Fun, isn't it?"

Marybeth had to admit it was.

Darla smiled. "Did you have a bra tree this morning?"

"A what?"

"A bra tree. There's always somebody in each cabin who gathers up all the bras and decorates a tree outside with them. If nobody in your cabin has thought of it, why don't you do it tomorrow?"

"I think I will." Marybeth thought about the way Petra had made the ghost last night and everybody except Marybeth had laughed about it. They'd laugh about the bra tree, too. She hoped Sam wouldn't be going past their cabin at the wrong time, though. "Thanks for telling me," she said.

Darla punched her arm lightly. "What are big sisters for? Now let's go practice our skit. Janine and Loni and I made it up last night."

Janine and Loni were Laurels, like Darla. They were all very clever, and the skit was fun. Its title was "Is That You Singing or Did Somebody Step on the Cat?" There were a lot of silly songs in it, and everybody got to say one or two speeches. Marybeth was sure their skit would be the very best one.

They hadn't quite finished rehearsing when Sam peered around the corner of a cabin. The branch was still stuck in his shirt and the leaves around his neck.

"I know I'm supposed to be, y'know, just a tree," he said, "but there's a telephone message for Darla and Marybeth." He beckoned to them. "You're supposed to call home."

Marybeth's heart skipped a beat. "Call home? What's happened?"

Darla looked scared too.

Sam shook his head. "It's not bad news," he said. "Your mom said it's, y'know, something good."

Darla turned to tell Loni to take over the rehearsal, and Marybeth joined Sam.

"Thanks," he whispered. "About the, y'know, snake. For not telling people, I mean."

Marybeth nodded. "Everybody's afraid of something."

Sam ducked his head, and Marybeth knew he was embarrassed.

"I used to wear that stick-on snake tattoo to see if I could, y'know, get over it," he confessed.

Marybeth remembered how he'd ripped it off after Garth and Grant scared him about Norman.

"Come look at the little snake I caught later," she said. "Maybe you'll like him."

Darla was coming. Sam gave Marybeth a grin and dashed off, his leaves rustling as he ran.

"Let's go," Darla said. She looked as if she wasn't all that sure the news from home would be good.

There were two telephones in the office, and the camp secretary let Darla and Marybeth each use one so they could both talk to their mother at the same time. "We don't have a lot of incoming calls," she said, "so it's okay."

Darla punched in a number and asked for a collect call. Pretty soon Mom's voice came on the phone.

"Hi, girls," she said. "Dad said I should call to tell you my good news."

Marybeth's heart resumed its steady beat. So it really *was* good news.

"What is it?" Both she and Darla spoke at once.

Mom took a deep breath. "I sold a story!" she said triumphantly.

Marybeth looked over at Darla, and Darla looked at her. What was Mom talking about?

"A story!" Mom repeated. "You know. A magazine story. I wrote it and they bought it."

"You mean, like you're, y'know, an author?" Marybeth couldn't head off that y'know. She still did it when she didn't know what to say.

"That's right," Mom said.

"That's what you were doing up in the tree?" Marybeth said. "Writing a story?"

"Yes," Mom said. "I didn't tell anybody about it because I was afraid."

Afraid? Mom afraid? Unflappable Mom who had a bumper sticker on her car that read "I can handle anything, I have children"—she was afraid?

"Afraid of failure," Mom went on to explain. "I studied writing in college. But that was eight kids ago. It's been so long. I thought I'd lost it. I went up in the tree to get away from everybody and kind of get a different perspective on things, to see them in a different way. That's what my story is about." She hesitated. "I went up in the tree because I didn't want anybody to see what I was doing in case I failed."

"Hey, Mom, congratulations." Darla had recovered her voice.

"Congratulations," Marybeth echoed. "I can't wait to read your story."

"It will be published in a magazine," Mom said with wonder. "They're actually paying me for it!"

"Wow!" Darla and Marybeth said together.

They hugged each other after they'd said good-bye and hung up. It seemed the right thing to do.

"How about that?" Darla said. "Mom's off on a new career."

"She was *afraid*." Marybeth still couldn't get over that part. It seemed as if everybody was *afraid* of something. Of failure. Of speaking in front of people. Of being in a cabin without your friends. Of lightning. Of snakes. Of love, even.

But none of those things was as babyish as being afraid of the dark.

By dinnertime, the storm was really bad. The wind shooshed through the pine trees, rattling the windowpanes in the dining hall. There were bright flashes of lightning, followed by crashes of thunder.

Rosaline was pale and quiet, but everyone else tried to ignore the storm. The older girls were being really hard on the younger ones about table manners.

When Becca leaned forward to talk to someone, several older girls started singing, *"Becca, Becca, if you're able, get your elbows off the table, this is not a horse's stall you know . . . "*

There was more. They sang, *"Around the mess hall you must go, you must go, you must go. Around the mess hall you must go. Learn your manners!"*

Becca grinned as she got up and ran around the mess hall. She didn't put her elbows on the table anymore, but another girl didn't hold her fork correctly and another didn't break her bread in half before eating it. They both got sung to and had to run around the mess hall.

It was fun, and it made everybody aware of how they were eating.

After dinner all the campers were requested to stay in the dining hall until the storm calmed down a little. That was okay with Marybeth. It was almost totally dark outside because of the black clouds, and she didn't want to go out there.

For entertainment they had a newspaper-costume contest where they were divided into groups of five, and each group dressed up one of its girls in newspapers, creating whatever kind of costume they wanted.

Marybeth's group chose her to be the model. They dressed her as a bride, folding and cutting and pinning newspapers until she stood there in a long, flowing paper dress with a veil.

One group of girls dressed their model as a rock star, with a weird top and a short skirt. Another model became a dinosaur, with a long, stuffed tail.

Still another wore a Scarlett O'Hara dress like in the movie *Gone with the Wind*.

And then there was a ghost. The ghost had huge, hollow black eyes, drawn on with a Marks-A-Lot pen.

They were lining up for a parade of newspaper costumes when, without warning, the lights went out.

Marybeth gasped in the sudden blackness.

"Somebody get a flashlight," a voice called.

Marybeth heard someone stumbling across the floor. Someone else giggled nervously. The paper costumes rattled as the girls wearing them moved.

Suddenly a brilliant flash of lightning illuminated the faces of the girls. They looked blue and bloodless. A whole room full of ghosts.

Thunder crashed.

Marybeth felt as if she were trapped in a nightmare. Her heart whammed against her ribs, making her paper costume whisper, "Ghost, ghost, ghost." Where was the light? She didn't want to, but she knew she was going to scream.

Twice she screamed. "Turn on a light," she shrieked. "I'm afraid of the dark."

Now everybody knew it. She didn't care. She tried to run toward where she thought a doorway was, but collided with something. Another flash of lightning showed something huge, with spreading arms, waiting to snatch her away.

"I'm afraid," she shrieked again.

She felt a hand slip into hers, and Becca's voice sang, *"Marybeth has a great big fear."*

"Did you hear?" That was Sunshine.

The Bee Theres were coming to her rescue.

"Great big fear, did you hear?" a lot of girls sang.

"Marybeth has a great big fear, and we all love her so."

There was laughter, and then Marybeth heard Rosaline's voice, thin and quavery, yell, "Rosaline is afraid of thunder."

Somebody picked it up. *"Why, I wonder?"* And everybody sang, *"Afraid of thunder. Why, I wonder? Rosaline is afraid of thunder, and we all love her so."*

"Afraid of snakes." That was Sam's voice. He and Quincy must have come in from the kitchen. He must have decided that if Marybeth could confess her fear, he'd tell his.

"Afraid of snakes," the girls sang. *"Heaven's sakes. Sam, he is afraid of snakes, and we all love him so."*

Somebody turned on a light at that moment, shining it on Sam, who blushed behind his leaves.

Marybeth saw that the huge thing she'd bumped into was just the girl dressed as a dinosaur. She also saw that all the Bee Theres had come over to surround her. Other girls turned to her, now that they could see.

"That was smart," someone said, "to start a song. It kept us all from being afraid."

"Marybeth, you're so great to think of that," someone else said.

They thought she'd yelled out just to keep everybody calm. That couldn't have been further from the truth. "I was scared," she confessed.

"I was too," somebody else said, and there were a dozen echoes of "I was too."

Nobody was making fun of her. Why had she ever thought they would? Everybody was afraid of something, weren't they? Hadn't she said that very thing to Sam? Even Garth and Grant, her goofy twin brothers, were afraid of something: afraid of speaking in public. But they'd gone ahead and done it, and it hadn't been so bad after all.

Maybe that's the way fear was. When you faced right up to it, maybe it was like the snake at girl's camp. According to all the stories, Norman was supposed to be huge and hideous, but he'd turned out to be a harmless little garter snake.

The lights in the dining hall came on as suddenly as they'd gone off. Everybody blinked and looked relieved. Lightning flashed and the thunder rolled outside, but even Rosaline was laughing now.

From across the room Marybeth saw Sam grinning at her. He raised one hand with his thumb and forefinger forming a circle, as if to say, "All *right,* Marybeth."

Then he raised the other arm and pointed to a long, green snake he'd drawn on his arm. Underneath he'd printed "Norman."

With a rustle of his leaves, he disappeared into the kitchen with Quincy. That was all right. They'd be talking more when they got home, when he didn't have to be a tree anymore. Maybe they could work together on getting rid of their "y'knows."

Outside, rain began to pelt the roof. It gave the big room kind of a cozy feeling.

Marybeth felt happy. It was so much fun being there with the other girls. And she and the other Bee Theres had Pamela's wedding to look forward to when they got back home!

"We're all here at Cougar Camp," Marybeth sang out suddenly.

"Cold and damp," somebody yelled.

And everybody sang, *"Cougar Camp, cold and damp. We're all here at Cougar Camp, and we all love it so."*

When Lael Littke was a Beehive girl in Mink Creek, Idaho, she loved to ride her horse and dream of someday living in a big city where she would be a writer. Now that she lives in Pasadena, California, and has written and published more than two dozen books, she loves to remember those wonderful days when she was young. She enjoys associating with the young people of her ward in Pasadena, California, and relies on them for ideas for her books. She has one daughter and a houseful of dogs and cats.